MODERN WORLD NATIONS

Portugal

Charles F. Gritzner
and
Douglas A. Phillips

Series Editor
Charles F. Gritzner
South Dakota State University

CHELSEA HOUSE
PUBLISHERS
An imprint of Infobase Publishing

This book is gratefully dedicated to the memory of those educators who instilled in the authors a lifelong love of learning and the desire to share their knowledge of the world's people and environments with others.

Frontispiece: Flag of Portugal

Cover: Wine boat, or rabelo, on Douro River, Porto, Portugal

Portugal

Copyright © 2007 by Infobase Publishing

All rights reserved. No part of this book may be reproduced or utilized in any form or by any means, electronic or mechanical, including photocopying, recording, or by any information storage or retrieval systems, without permission in writing from the publisher. For information contact:

Chelsea House
An imprint of Infobase Publishing
132 West 31st Street
New York NY 10001

Library of Congress Cataloging-in-Publication Data
Phillips, Douglas A.
  Portugal / Douglas A. Phillips and Charles F. Gritzner.
    p. cm. — (Modern world nations)
  Includes bibliographical references and index.
  ISBN-13: 978-0-7910-9257-6 (hardcover)
  ISBN-10: 0-7910-9257-7 (hardcover)
  1. Portugal—Juvenile literature.   I. Gritzner, Charles F.   II. Title.   III. Series.

  DP517.P45 2007
  946.9—dc22

2007000989

Chelsea House books are available at special discounts when purchased in bulk quantities for businesses, associations, institutions, or sales promotions. Please call our Special Sales Department in New York at (212) 967-8800 or (800) 322-8755.

You can find Chelsea House on the World Wide Web at http://www.chelseahouse.com

Series and cover design by Takeshi Takahashi

Printed in the United States of America

Bang NMSG 10 9 8 7 6 5 4 3 2 1

This book is printed on acid-free paper.

All links and Web addresses were checked and verified to be correct at the time of publication. Because of the dynamic nature of the Web, some addresses and links may have changed since publication and may no longer be valid.

Table of Contents

Portugal

1

Introducing Portugal

Precariously perched on the westernmost coast of mainland Europe lies the nation of Portugal—a country on the move. This small country's location near the Mediterranean Sea and facing the vast expanse of the Atlantic Ocean has served it well.

For centuries, Portugal has turned to the sea: to fish, to explore, to colonize, to trade, and recently, even to generate electrical power. The country is perhaps best known as a launching place for early explorers and their many achievements and discoveries. From Portugal's ports, brave navigators departed on their journeys into uncharted waters as they explored the world. Names like Vasco da Gama, Ferdinand Magellan, Bartolomeu Dias, and Pedro Álvares Cabral resonate in the pages of world history as Portugal staked its claim as a world power. The adventuresome spirit, fostered by the creative intelligence of Prince Henry the Navigator and many brave explorers, created a maritime heritage that is more pronounced than the land area and population of Portugal would be thought to merit.

Although small in both size and population, Portugal is a giant in terms of its history and culture. From the explorers and discoverers to the magical, mystical, multicolored castle at Sintra, and to the beautiful beaches and rugged coastal shores, the country is filled with intrigue, captivating stories, and breathtaking scenery. From modern Lisbon to rural villages and agricultural landscapes, the country has used its environment in countless ways that are practical and often innovative.

Portugal is a small country by world standards. It has a land area of only 35,672 square miles (92,391 square kilometers), which is smaller than the state of Indiana or slightly larger than Canada's New Brunswick province. According to estimates by the U.S. Central Intelligence Agency (CIA), Portugal had a population of 10,605,870 in 2006. This compares to a 2005 population estimate of 6,271,973 for Indiana. Thus, Portugal does not have either a huge land area or a large population from which to draw natural or human resources. These two basic factors beg the question of how such a small country can have such an incredible history and culture. This book will explain how tiny Portugal's reach has been so great.

WHERE IS PORTUGAL?

Looking at a map, it is easy to see that Portugal's location is somewhat unique. Located on the Iberian Peninsula, it has only one land neighbor—Spain. These neighbors share a 754-mile (1,214-kilometer) border, as well as a history that has been marked by periods of conflict, competition, and occasional cooperation. With air travel connections today, Portugal is also near the United Kingdom—the capitals of the two historical sea powers are only 983 miles (1,582 kilometers) apart.

One of the keys to understanding Portugal's expanded role on the world stage is its access to the sea. Located on the Atlantic Ocean, the country has a 1,114-mile (1,793-kilometer) coastline.

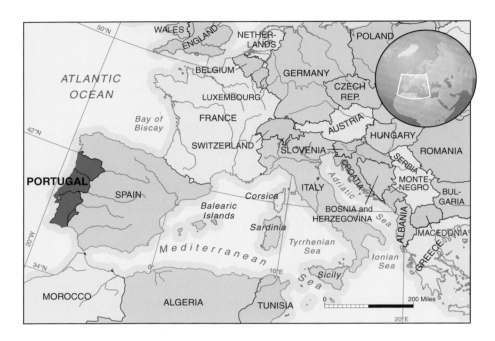

One of the smallest nations in western Europe, Portugal is located on the Iberian Peninsula and only shares a border with one country–Spain. Due to its proximity to the Atlantic Ocean, Portugal has been intimately tied to the sea throughout its history.

Proximity to and use of the sea has made it possible for the country to prosper. Think of Portugal as being in a strategic location that connects the sea and the land—two-thirds of the country is bordered by the Atlantic Ocean, allowing easy access to the rest of the world. The other third of the country's border is land that connects Portugal to the countries and peoples of the Eurasian land mass. The sea has helped to nurture Portugal with food, colonies, trade, entertainment, and a variety of other elements that developed alongside Portuguese ingenuity and bravery.

Enhancing Portugal's maritime location are the many rivers that run through the country. Portugal has 10 major rivers, most of which flow westward into the Atlantic from highlands located inland. Five of the rivers actually originate in Spain, while the other five start in Portugal. *Rio* is the word used in both Portuguese and Spanish for river. The beautiful Rio Douro is lined with terraced vineyards and serves as an important artery for economic activity in the north. In the south, the Rio Guadiana partially serves as a border between Portugal and Spain and as the region's most important river. The Rio Guadiana is also a rare exception in Portugal in that it flows southward.

The most important river in Portugal, however, is the mighty Rio Tejo, also called the River Tagus. This river has its source in the Sierra de Albarracin in Spain. The Tagus estuary provides Lisbon with the most outstanding natural port in Europe. Even the largest ships can easily navigate and dock in Lisbon's huge natural harbor. This port has had great historical importance and today is vital as an economic hub for the country. The dry docks in the parish of Cacilhas, located on the Tagus River in Lisbon, are the world's largest. In addition to its historical and contemporary importance, the Tagus also serves to divide the country into northern and southern cultural regions. North of the river, many people have Celtic and Germanic roots. South of the river, the Mediterranean, Moorish, and Roman influences are stronger. Agriculture also differs. The north has more traditional crops, including potatoes, grains, and corn, whereas the south produces crops more fitting a Mediterranean climate, such as oranges, figs, olives, and cork oak.

But the sea is the key. Inside Lisbon's harbor lies a small district called Belém. This is the place in the city where most Portuguese explorers began their journeys into the unknown. Today a visitor to Belém will see the visually striking Monument to the Discoveries. This 170-foot-high (52 meters) monument was created in 1960 to celebrate the 500th anniversary of Prince Henry the Navigator's death. The beautiful tribute depicts Prince Henry leading the way with his bold vision, while Ferdinand Magellan, Vasco da Gama, Pedro Alvares Cabral, and other Portuguese follow. On the large walkway beside the monument, a huge compass and map is cut into the stone. The map shows the routes of

The Monument to the Discoveries is one of Lisbon's most famous landmarks. Dedicated in 1960, during the celebrations of the 500th anniversary of Prince Henry the Navigator's death, the monument commemorates Portugal's seafaring heritage.

discoverers and the range of the far-flung Portuguese explorations. A few blocks away there is a fascinating maritime museum that documents the country's exploits. A few footsteps from the museum are the tombs of Vasco da Gama and others. The symbol of Lisbon and perhaps all of Portugal is also in Belém: the famous Belém Tower, built during the era of Portuguese exploration.

Peering over Lisbon Harbor—almost as if he were blessing Portugal's sea prowess with his outstretched hands—is a statue of Jesus Christ. He is portrayed on a towering 369-foot-high (111 meters) statue and pedestal called Cristo Rei. The statue is patterned after the famed Christ the Redeemer statue in Rio de Janeiro, Brazil. From the statue's position, a visitor can see most of Lisbon's harbor. Below, the activities linking land and sea are conducted at a busy pace. Tankers, ferries, cars, trucks, trains, cruise ships, and other forms of transportation serve to link the land of modern Portugal to the sea.

However, there are many more stories to tell. This chapter has only been a small snapshot of Portugal. An entire album of images and information lies ahead on this exploration and voyage of geographic discovery into Portugal's past, present, and future.

2

Physical Landscapes

P hysical geography includes the landforms, weather and climate, plant and animal life, water features, soils, and mineral resources of a place. All of these factors form the stage upon which human activities are played out. Nature, of course, does not determine the ways humans use, avoid, or perhaps misuse their environmental surroundings. Culture—a people's needs, values, perceptions, technology, finances, and other factors—establishes the link between humans and the physical environment. Portugal, like all countries, has been both blessed and limited by its natural features and conditions.

This chapter will focus on Portugal's natural environment and the ways in which the Portuguese have taken advantage of nature's offerings throughout time. The following chapters will reveal how they have culturally adapted to, used, and modified the land on which they live.

IBERIA: A PENINSULA ON A PENINSULA

Europe has been called a "peninsula of peninsulas." The continent's core is little more than a relatively small, westward-jutting peninsular extension of the huge Eurasian landmass. Extending from this core is a series of other peninsulas: the Scandinavian, Jutland (Denmark), Balkan (Greece), Apennine (Italian), and Iberian. The Iberian Peninsula juts in a southwesterly direction from mainland western Europe. It is bordered by the Mediterranean Sea in eastern Spain, and the Atlantic Ocean in portions of Spain and all of coastal Portugal. The peninsula is somewhat isolated from the remainder of Europe by the Pyrenees Mountains, which tower to elevations above 11,000 feet (3,353 meters). This isolation has encouraged both the Spaniards and the Portuguese to turn outward toward the sea, rather than inward toward mainland Europe. It has also tightly woven together their histories in numerous ways. The Portuguese, in particular, have used the sea to their advantage for centuries.

THE COUNTRY OF PORTUGAL

Physically, Portugal is an elongated country. It stretches from about 37° to 42° north latitude, a distance slightly less than 400 miles (650 kilometers). Its average width from east to west is about 100 miles (160 kilometers). Portugal's mainland territory lies roughly between 7° and 9° west longitude. This makes it mainland Europe's only country that lies entirely in the Western Hemisphere. (The island countries of Ireland and Iceland also are wholly within the Western Hemisphere.) In fact, with the Portuguese Autonomous Region of Azores, Portugal is the westernmost country in all of Europe. The Azorean Archipelago (island chain) lies in the Atlantic Ocean, hundreds of miles farther west than Iceland (and approximately 1,000 miles west of mainland Portugal).

Portugal also lies quite close to the center of what geographers call the "Land and People Hemisphere." Take a globe and position it so that Paris, France, is at the center of the

Portugal stretches approximately 400 miles (650 kilometers) north to south but is only about 100 miles (160 kilometers) in width. Most of Portugal's landscape can best be described as gently rolling, but there are mountains in the eastern and northern sections of the country, especially north of the Rio Douro.

hemisphere in view. This hemisphere (half of the globe) has about 85 percent of Earth's land area and is home to some 90 percent of the human population. Portugal's location in relation to the world's land and people puts the country in a very favorable, central spot for trade and other activities in which distance is a factor.

LAND FEATURES

Most of Portugal consists of lowlands and hills. This is particularly true of the gently rolling, low-lying terrain found throughout the southern half of the country. Coastal and river flood plains and other relatively flat lands dominate the landscape there. In the absence of major barriers, transportation routes find easy access. In the north, elevations are higher and the terrain becomes somewhat more rugged. Low mountains, large areas of rugged plateau, and the occasional deep valley offer a sharp contrast to the rather featureless topography of the south. The highest elevation in mainland Portugal is 6,539 feet (1,993 meters) in the Serra da Estrela. This elevation is slightly lower than North Carolina's Mount Mitchell, the highest point in the Appalachian Mountains.

Portugal's other autonomous region, the Madeira Archipelago, is composed of eight islands, only two of which are inhabited. The landscape of this island chain is generally rugged. Mountainous Madeira Island is the largest of the group, with an area of about 300 square miles (777 square kilometers). It also has the archipelago's highest elevation, rising to 6,109 feet (1,862 meters). The Azores form an archipelago that includes nine islands, many of which were formed by volcanic activity. Pico Alto (also called Ponta do Pico), located in the Azores, is Portugal's highest point. Its elevation, 7,713 feet (2,351 meters), is comparable to Harney Peak, the highest point in South Dakota's Black Hills, and for that matter, all of Northern America east of the Rocky Mountains.

WEATHER AND CLIMATE

If superimposed over the West Coast of the United States, Portugal would more or less stretch from central Oregon to San Francisco, California. Portugal's weather (day-to-day atmospheric conditions) and climate (long-term average weather) are also quite similar to those experienced along the West Coast of the United States. Southern Portugal enjoys a relatively mild and very pleasant Mediterranean climate, similar to that of coastal Southern California. In the north, conditions are considerably wetter. There, the temperate marine climate resembles conditions that occur farther north along the coasts of northern California and Oregon.

As is the case along the West Coast of the United States, temperatures are quite mild throughout most of Portugal. In fact, it is one of Europe's warmest countries. Because of the country's closeness to the moderating influence of the sea, temperature extremes are rare. In the south, the annual average temperature in Fahrenheit is in the mid-60s (17° to 18°C). Only rarely will temperatures climb above 100°F (38°C). Freezing temperatures are also very rare and have never occurred in some low-lying coastal locations. Northern Portugal is somewhat cooler, both during the summer and winter, because of its more northerly latitude and higher elevations. The yearly temperature averages there are in the mid-50s (12° to 14°C) in most locations. On average, temperatures drop about 3.5°F with each 1,000-foot increase in elevation (6.5°C per 1,000 meters) under normal atmospheric conditions. In the highlands, freezing temperatures are more common and snow occasionally blankets the land.

Precipitation varies greatly from south to north. In the south, summers are generally cloudless and very dry, much as they are in Southern California. In the Algarve region in the far south of Portugal, some areas receive less than 10 inches (25 centimeters) of precipitation each year, resulting in quite parched, semidesert conditions. Throughout most of southern

The volcanic Madeira Islands are located off the southwestern coast of Portugal and consist of two inhabited and six uninhabited islands. Pictured here is Porto Santo Island, which is the smaller of the two inhabited islands.

Portugal, however, 20 to 40 inches (50 to 100 centimeters) of rain falls each year, nearly all of it during the winter months. Conditions are much different in the north, which receives an annual average of 40 to 60 inches (100 to 150 centimeters) of moisture. Some mountain locations receive as much as 100 inches (250 centimeters) of precipitation, some of which falls as snow at higher elevations. There, as in the south, most precipitation is received during the winter months. Islands of both the Madeira and the Azores chains enjoy mild temperatures and 25 to 45 inches (64 to 114 centimeters) of precipitation annually. The Madeira Islands have a balmy Mediterranean climate, characterized by a lack of temperature extremes and a very dry summer. The Azores, much like northern Portugal, experience a temperate marine climate with a more even seasonal distribution of rain and slightly cooler temperatures. During the winter, in fact, the Azores often experience quite chilly and blustery weather.

In summary, conditions of weather and climate are generally pleasant throughout all of Portugal. Temperature and precipitation offer few challenges to either human settlement or most types of economic activity. Many people, in fact, regard the Mediterranean climate as being the most pleasant in the world. In terms of human use and comfort, it is followed closely by the mild and moist conditions of the temperate marine climate.

PLANT AND ANIMAL LIFE

Humans have occupied the land that is now Portugal for tens of thousands of years. As a result, little of the original natural vegetation remains. Many animals, too, have given way over time to the expanding human population. As is true in much of the heavily populated areas of the world, domesticated livestock and poultry have replaced wildlife. In most places, pastures and fields of crops have replaced natural vegetation, thereby further reducing wildlife habitat.

In the south, much of the natural vegetation is Mediterranean *chaparral,* very similar to the type of plant cover common in much of Southern California. Chaparral is characterized by dense, scrubby, broad-leaved evergreen bushes, shrubs, and low trees. Common species include several types of oak, including the cork oak for which the country is famous. Wild olives and several varieties of pine also thrive. Because the region receives more precipitation, northern Portugal is more densely forested.

Chestnut, elm, poplar, several species of pine and oak, and wild olive are common there. In many locations throughout Portugal, varieties of eucalyptus also thrive. This hardy, fast-growing tree was introduced to the area from its native Australia about a century ago. Today, Portugal is attempting to protect at least some of its remaining natural vegetation. The country has established a number of national parks, nature preserves, and national forests.

Portugal's wild animals are a mix of North African and European species. Wild goats, pigs, and deer roam more remote mountainous areas, as do wolves and lynx. Foxes, hares, and rabbits are found throughout most of the country. Birdlife is abundant. Not only are there a number of native species, but also the Iberian Peninsula lies astride major seasonal migration routes. Waters of the Atlantic Ocean teem with fish, especially sardines. Crustaceans and oyster beds are common to many coastal zones and river estuaries.

WATER FEATURES

Historically, Portuguese culture has revolved around the sea. The Atlantic Ocean has played a very important role in the country's exploration, colonial expansion, and economy. There is some evidence to support a belief that Portuguese fishermen crossed the Atlantic to fish the waters of eastern Canada's Grand Banks long before Columbus's epic voyage in the late 1400s. The well-documented European voyages of discovery received a tremendous boost from the efforts of Portugal's Prince Henry in the fifteenth century. His school of navigation, begun during the second decade of the fifteenth century, greatly advanced shipbuilding, sail design, and navigational technology. Later, the Portuguese followed sea routes to discover, explore, and ultimately colonize lands in what became a far-flung empire.

Portugal has very little fresh surface water. There are few lakes or reservoirs and the rivers are quite small. The largest river is the Douro, which, like most of the country's other rivers, flows from Spain. The Douro crosses northern Portugal and reaches the Atlantic at Porto (Oporto), the country's second-largest city. In the far southeast, the Guadiana River forms part of Portugal's boundary with Spain. The stream flows across the country's driest region. In 2002, what became Europe's largest reservoir (man-made lake) began to fill behind the huge Alqueva Dam. Water from the reservoir is used to irrigate the parched fields of southern Portugal. The dam also produces hydroelectric power, and the lake is being developed as a tourist attraction. Lisbon, Portugal's capital and largest city, in addition to being a major seaport, is located at the point where the Tagus River flows into the country's and Europe's finest natural harbor.

NATURAL RESOURCES

Portugal is not well endowed with natural resources. There are small deposits of copper, zinc, tin, and iron ore, and small amounts of silver and gold have been found. Additionally, there are commercially developed deposits of marble, clay, gypsum, and salt. Mineral fuels, however, are lacking. The country must import all of its coal, petroleum, and natural gas, a factor that places a tremendous burden on its economy.

There are some natural resources for which Portugal is well known. Forests of cork oak have supplied much of the world's cork supply, and both wild and domestic olives flourish throughout much of the country. Nearly one-fifth of Portugal has soils adequate for farming, and a much larger area is suited to livestock grazing. Many rivers, including the Guadiana's recent Alqueva Dam project, provide hydro-electric energy. Portuguese fishermen have long turned to the sea as a valuable source of protein, and the coastal zone produces abundant harvests of shellfish. Portugal also can boast of having many wonderful beaches, more than 100 in the Algarve region alone.

NATURAL HAZARDS

Natural hazards affect Portugal in a variety of ways, some of which are atmospheric and others geologic in origin. Fortunately, loss of life resulting from catastrophic natural events is rare. Each year, however, nature takes its toll on property and the country's landscape.

Weather Related Hazards

By and large, severe storms are limited to the Madeira and Azores island groups that lie in the path of Atlantic hurricanes. Because of their location, however, they are not as vulnerable as are islands of the Caribbean. Most years pass with little if any hurricane damage. Occasionally, a passing storm or infrequent direct hit will cause wind damage and local flooding. At opposite ends of the precipitation scale, both severe droughts and devastating floods plague Portugal. During 2005, the country experienced its worst drought in more than 50 years. Normally lush vegetation became a parched landscape of yellow and brown as flora withered away and huge fires charred vast areas. A year later, in late October 2006, heavy rains left much of central Portugal under floodwater. The torrents of rain also triggered mudslides that caused widespread damage. Occurrences such as these are quite common on the Iberian Peninsula.

As anyone living in Southern California knows, wildfires are commonplace during the summer and early autumn months. Such fires occur frequently in those areas of the world that experience the summer drought that is characteristic of the Mediterranean climate. In the Northern Hemisphere, the June through October period is generally very dry and the hottest season of the year. Under these conditions, Mediterranean vegetation becomes dry and brittle. A simple spark can turn the chaparral into a raging inferno in a matter of minutes. The intense heat of the flames often generates a raging firestorm—flames carried by heat-created winds that can reach hurricane force and sweep across the terrain, devouring everything in their path.

Like the Madeira Islands to the south, the Azores are also volcanic in origin. Located approximately 1,000 miles (1,600 kilometers) west of mainland Portugal, the Azores are made up of nine islands, including Pico Island, which is home to the archipelago's largest volcano—Ponta do Pico.

Geologic Hazards

Volcanic eruptions occur occasionally in the Azores and earthquakes can rattle both the Madeira Islands and Azores. Coastal Portugal also is subject to potentially destructive tsunamis (often mistakenly called "tidal waves"). These massive waves are caused by seismic shocks, huge mudslides or earthslides, or volcanic eruptions that occur on the floor of the Atlantic

Ocean. Tsunamis can sweep ashore with tremendous force and devastate beaches, coastal villages, and other landscape features of the coastal zone.

In Portugal, no natural disaster can come close to matching the devastation of the earthquake that struck Lisbon on November 1, 1755. That event was one of the strongest, most destructive, and deadliest earthquakes in history. Just before 10 in the morning on the day of the Catholic holiday of All Saints' Day, Portugal's largest city was struck by a huge tremor. Scientists estimate that the quake would have measured at least magnitude 9.0 on the Richter scale (which had not yet been developed). The earth shook wildly for as long as six minutes. Buildings were toppled, streets buckled, and hillsides were swept away. Giant fissures opened the earth, leaving yawning gaps 16-feet (5 meters) wide at the heart of the city.

No sooner had the earth stopped trembling than an earthquake-triggered tsunami roared into the harbor and up the Tagus River. It was followed by several more huge waves that swept across the harbor and downtown area, leaving total devastation in their wake. But the destruction was not over. When the tsunamis subsided, a raging fire broke out in non-flooded areas. Flames soon consumed much of the remaining parts of the city. By the time the catastrophe had ended, an estimated 100,000 of Lisbon's 275,000 inhabitants had died and about 85 percent of the city lay in ruin. The loss of historic buildings, art, library collections, statues, tombs, and other treasures was inestimable. It was a tragic event that had a profound impact on the country's future.

The following chapter continues this voyage through the corridors of time, through Portugal's sometimes romantic, occasionally turbulent, and always amazing history. Discover the ways in which Portugal—a small country in both size and population—for a time came to be a fabulously rich, major world power.

3

Portugal
Through Time

H istory has shown that Portugal's location on the Atlantic
Ocean has been both a blessing and a curse. While the sea
has provided ready access to the world for this nation of
explorers, it has also provided a wide avenue for foreigners to access
the peninsula. This access has often been used with the intent of
conquering the Iberian Peninsula and implementing political control
over its people. Because of their location, many events in history have
closely tied the fates of Spain and Portugal together. The physical
geography tended to blend the histories of the two countries, rather
than divide them. In the absence of major barriers, the Iberian Peninsula, made up of the lands south of the Pyrenees Mountains, was a
relatively open and easily traversed terrain. With easy access between
both Portugal and Spain, armies, traders, and marauders were not
stopped at the border that eventually developed between them. Thus

when the Romans, Moors, and others moved by land or sea onto the peninsula, both countries were often affected in a similar manner.

The story of the Portuguese is an amazing tale that can be traced from the first early peoples to invasions by foreigners, to a world sea power, to a dictatorship, and finally to a modern democratic member of the European Union. Often lost in the tales of other larger European countries, Portugal has an amazing story that must not be forgotten. It is a tale filled with adventure, scandals, kings and queens, betrayal, murder, rivalries, dictators, and other events that will be related in this chapter. The story of Portugal told here will follow the path this country and its charming people have taken in their journey over time to become the vibrant exciting country that exists today.

THE FIRST PORTUGUESE

Establishing who were the earliest people in a region and when they arrived is never an easy task. In pre-history (the time before written history), evidence needs to be gathered in ways other than book research. This means that determining the earliest dates and people in a region are usually established by the findings of anthropologists and archaeologists who have discovered traces of humans. These traces may be human bones or teeth, pottery, tools, drawings on cave walls, or a number of other elements that provide evidence about early people and their culture. Evidence suggests that the earliest people in Portugal existed nearly one-half million years ago, with Neanderthals appearing first, and later, *Homo sapiens* (modern humans).

Recent research indicates that the last of the Neanderthals may have existed in Portugal and Gibraltar, where they disappeared about 28,000 years ago. Or did they? In 1998, the remains of a young four- or five-year-old boy were found in a shallow grave 90 miles north of Lisbon. The skeleton

In 1994, the world's largest open-air collection of rock carvings were discovered in northern Portugal. The carvings date from the Upper Palaeolithic (22,000 to 10,000 B.C.) period and were designated a World Heritage Site in 1998 by the United Nations Educational, Scientific, and Cultural Organization (UNESCO). Pictured here is archaeologist Martinho Baptista, who is pointing to a carving that shows two horses mating.

was about 24,500 years old. This was no ordinary boy. DNA research conducted by Dr. João Zilhao, director of the Institute of Archaeology in Lisbon, indicated that the boy was a cross-breed between Neanderthals and Cro-Magnons (a forerunner of modern humans). This astonishing find created a major stir in the world of archaeology, as Cro-Magnons were not known to have mixed with Neanderthals, who had disappeared 4,000 years earlier. A controversy was ignited.

Evidence of early peoples also turned up in other unex-pected ways. For example, the Coa River valley near Moncorvo was slated to become a reservoir when the river was dammed. The project was abandoned, however, when a large array of rock engravings was discovered. This art work turned out to be the largest open-air collection of rock paintings in the world dating from the Stone Age era. Today the region is preserved and has been designated a World Heritage Site by UNESCO (the United Nations Educational, Scientific, and Cultural Orga-nization). Visitors can now view this fragile ancient art at the Parque Arqueologico do Vale Coa.

At the end of the Paleolithic period, around 8,000 to 7,000 B.C., the valley of the Tagus River was inhabited by people who primarily fished and hunted. Evidence of these civiliza-tions has mainly come from burial and waste disposal sites. In disposal sites, the bones of deer, sheep, horses, wild dogs, pigs, and other animals have been found, along with evidence of shellfish and other sea animals.

Evidence indicates that a Neolithic agricultural society emerged later, around 3,000 B.C. Found in northern Portugal, these peoples cleared forests for farming. These farmers also left earthen construction burial grounds called megaliths that have served as an excellent source of information on their culture in Portugal. The megaliths in the Alentejo region in particular provide an example of what might be learned about this time period. It is believed that the Alentejo megalith was a temple where people worshipped. This belief is based on the fact that there is a relationship between parts of the megalith and the positions of major stars, specifically, a star cluster called the Pleiades. While the original purpose of this megalith is not clear, it is obvious that these early farmers possessed advanced knowledge for their time.

Regional cultural variations began to appear among Neolithic peoples around 2,000 B.C. Additional megaliths also appeared in locations such as Palmela, Alcalar, Reguengos, and Monsaraz, as the Neolithic period gave way to the Bronze and Iron ages. These eras brought the arrival of outsiders who settled on the Iberian Peninsula. Among these were the Ligures and the Iberos, who were believed to have come from North Africa. Little is known about the Ligures, but the Iberos had a system of writing and used plows and carts.

MORE PEOPLE ARRIVE BY SEA

The Phoenicians arrived into the area now known as Portugal in the twelfth century B.C. These traders roamed the Mediterranean region and portions of the Atlantic coast of Europe in search of commodities, particularly metals. They established trading posts along the southern and western coasts of Portugal, including one that was where the city of Lisbon is situated today. Other Phoenicians settled in the Algarve region in the south, where they passed on their fishing practices and boat styles, which reflect their influence.

The Phoenicians were hardly alone in investigating the wealth of possibilities in Portugal. In the east, the Celts arrived from central Europe in a series of migration waves between the sixth and eighth centuries B.C. These people were also interested in agriculture and prospered in the rich lands of Portugal. The Greeks also arrived in the seventh century B.C. and started settlements on both the Atlantic and Mediterranean coasts of Iberia.

As the new groups appeared, another foreign power was growing stronger and seemed poised to be the next group to invade the peninsula. Carthage, located in what is today Tunisia, was a rising power in the Mediterranean region. In the fifth century B.C., Carthaginians arrived in Portugal and pushed out the Phoenicians. They then attempted to lock out the Greeks by closing off the narrow Strait of Gibraltar. The Carthaginians proceeded to occupy much of the Iberian Peninsula. Some areas in the west and the north were not under their control, but Carthaginian rule continued throughout much of Portugal until the Romans arrived in the third century B.C.

THE ROMAN EMPIRE ABSORBS PORTUGAL

Rome was the next invader to arrive on the scene in Portugal. During the Second Punic War, which took place from 218 to 201 B.C., the Romans swept into Spain and Portugal and drove the Carthaginians from Spain. However, Portugal resisted, with the Lusitanian leader Viriato bravely leading his forces in guerrilla attacks against the invaders. The Lusitanians were an indigenous people who lived in western Portugal. The scrappy Lusitanians held off the Romans until 139 B.C., when Viriato was betrayed and murdered in his bed by three assassins who were paid henchmen of the Romans. Julius Caesar finalized the stamp of Roman power on Portugal in 60 B.C., when he arrived with a huge army. Only areas in the north were outside of Roman rule, instead remaining under the power of the Celts. Even though Viriato and the Lusitanians failed to resist the Romans, Viriato is recognized as the country's first hero for having led a brave resistance.

Roman rule lasted for about 500 years. The Romans tied Portugal and Spain together into a province within their ever-expanding empire. An administrative center for Portugal was created by the Romans and located in Olissipo, which later became Lisbon. Roman rule had many benefits, even if the Romans were foreigners. Rome's organizational and technological contributions served Portugal much the same as other areas of the Roman Empire. Excellent bridges, roads, and aqueducts

After the Roman Empire defeated Carthage in the Second Punic War
(218–201 B.C.), much of eastern and southern Portugal came under
Rome's purview. Roman influence quickly spread throughout the country,
and many Roman structures, such as the Temple of Diana in Evora, are
still around today.

were built. Amazingly, many of these are still around today. The
Roman language of Latin was extended across Portugal and
served as the foundation for the modern Portuguese language.
New crops such as wheat, olives, and barley were introduced; so
were the processes for making brick and tile. The Romans also
brought Christianity to the peninsula, and today 94 percent of
Portuguese are Catholic. Thus, the Romans had a huge impact
upon the development of Portugal, having introduced a wide
array of lasting cultural benefits and influences.

But another wave of invaders loomed on the horizon. As
the Roman Empire weakened, it became increasingly difficult

to control the lands scattered across its far-flung empire. When the Western Roman Empire was deteriorating in Europe, Germanic tribes and others moved onto the Iberian Peninsula, starting in A.D. 406. In an attempt to hold on to their waning power, the Romans hired the Visigoths to protect their interests in the region. The Visigoths, also Germanic, were Romanized to a large extent and maintained the Latin language and other Roman practices. As Rome weakened further, the Visigoths proceeded to create their own kingdom on the peninsula with their capital in the city of Toledo in Spain. Portugal was a part of this Visigoth kingdom.

In general, the Visigoths had minimal impact on the culture and people of the Iberian region, but they did strongly maintain and extend Christianity in their kingdom. Internal power struggles emerged in the early eighth century between the Visigoth leaders who attempted to succeed King Roderick. This led to a weakening of the Visigoths, who were under increasing pressure from the Moors of North Africa. As the Visigoths lay vulnerable, the Moors, fueled by the fervor of a rapidly spreading Islamic faith, were taking aim at the Iberian Peninsula from the south. This Moorish wave would prove to have a huge and lasting impact on Portugal, and would also foreshadow the continuing religious struggles between Christianity and Islam.

THE INFLUENCE OF THE MOORS

In A.D. 710, Tarif ibn Malluk commanded a band of 400 Moors. He led them from Ceuta in North Africa across the narrow Strait of Gibraltar in a successful attack on the southern part of the Iberian Peninsula. This event was a precursor to the larger invasion that followed in 711, when Tariq ibn Ziyad attacked with an army of 12,000 at the Rock of Gibraltar. King Roderick tried to resist, but was killed in battle. By 718, the Moors had conquered most of the peninsula and had given the region the Arabic name of Al Andalus. Christians only retained a small area in the northwest called Astúrias. Their hold on this area was partially due to the fact that the Moors did not like the cooler and more humid climate north of the Tagus River, and so did not actively try to conquer the region.

The Moors were not a singular group; rather, they were a composite of a number of North Africans who had fervor for the Islamic faith. Thus, the term *Moor* really refers to a wide range of Muslims, including an assortment of Arabs, Egyptian Copts, and Moroccan Berbers. The Islamic prophet Mohammad died in 632 and had ordered his followers to conduct a *jihad* (holy war) against those who did not follow Islam. This made the Moors one of the earliest agents of jihad as they headed toward Europe. The Moors arrived not only with their army, but also were armed with their new religion and a complex culture that they brought from North Africa.

Many lower-class Visigoths on the peninsula were not devout Christians, so a good deal of them converted to Islam. Some of the aristocrats, on the other hand, maintained their Christian beliefs, since the Moorish rulers were surprisingly tolerant of other religions. Nonetheless, many members of the upper class also became Muslims and even assumed positions of leadership in the Moorish government. Jews also lived in Portugal at the time and tended to focus on such activities as commerce and education.

Al Andalus prospered under the Muslim caliphs who ruled from their capital in Córdoba. The city, now located in Spain, was renowned for its wealth, culture, and beauty. This prosperity lasted for a quarter of a millennium, because the Moors introduced new ideas in mathematics, science, architecture, and the arts. They also introduced irrigation, crop rotation, and advanced mining and business interests on the peninsula. Important sea technology also came with the Moors, including such devices as the magnetic compass, astrolabe (used to determine latitude), and innovative ways of shipbuilding. In addition, the Moors added greatly to the Portuguese language. Today, many Portuguese toponyms (place names) are derived from the Arabic language, as are more than 600 Portuguese words.

After 500 years of rule, the Moors' power began to decline. It started when the region of Córdoba was divided into smaller city-states. During this period, small kingdoms, called *taifas*, like Lisbon, Badajoz, Mérida, and Évora, began to take shape. These smaller city-states were easier targets for Visigoth Christians. The Christians had been holding out for centuries in the mountainous stronghold at Astúrias. Their resistance had not faded, and they worked to regain the lands lost to the Moors. The Christian push toward the south and their eviction of the Moors had been going on for 200 years. It accelerated when Córdoba began to break up and when the Moors' influence began to weaken as the result of internal divisions.

During the Christian retaking of the Iberian Peninsula, the seeds of an independent Portugal were planted. In the early twelfth century, Teresa, an illegitimate daughter of Afonso VI, married Henry of Burgundy. Henry of Burgundy had helped Afonso VI to push the Moors southward, and he was rewarded with Teresa for his efforts. A part of her dowry (payment made by the bride's family to the groom) included the area then called Portucale. With the dowry, Henry became the ruler of Portucale. Teresa and Henry's son Afonso Henriques was born in 1109. Henry died five years later, and Teresa became the ruler of the region. At age 19, and after years of conflict and fighting with his mother, Afonso Henriques rebelled and took the throne from her. He then banished her into exile at Galicia, where she later died.

Afonso Henriques was the key figure in establishing the House of Burgundy in 1128, which initiated Portugal's first royal family. He led the Portuguese to an important victory over the Moors in the battle of Ourique in 1139. This further secured his leadership and soon afterward he was declared the king of Portugal. This ignited the ire of Alfonso VII, the emperor of León and Castile (modern Spain), who saw this as a rebel threat to his rule in the region. When Afonso Henriques asserted his claims to Galicia and invaded the region in 1140, Alfonso VII responded by attacking Portugal. The two armies met at Arcos de Valdevez and staged a jousting tournament on March 25, 1140. The Portuguese knights won the jousting match and Afonso Henriques received the Toronho region of Galicia. Alfonso VII still believed himself to be superior to Afonso Henriques, but in the Treaty of Zamora (1143), he recognized Portugal as a country independent of León and Castile. A representative of the Catholic pope served as a witness to validate the treaty.

As king of Portugal, Afonso Henriques, now called Afonso I, continued his battle against the Moors and in 1147 was successful in driving them out of Lisbon with the help of a group of Catholic crusaders. He had gained the backing of the pope and used this support in his efforts to drive the Moors out of much of the peninsula. He died in 1185, leaving only the Algarve and Alentejo regions under Moorish rule. Afonso III, who ruled the House of Burgundy from 1248 to 1279, completed the effort to remove the Moors from Portugal by capturing the last stronghold at the southern city of Faro in 1249. The area ruled by Portugal in 1249 is virtually the same as today's boundaries. The Christians had prevailed; Portugal was now a country and faced an uncertain future. How would Portugal proceed? Would it continue to be the victim of invaders, or would another path emerge?

UNIFYING THE COUNTRY

For much of Portugal's early history, the country seemed to be a doormat for other powers around the Mediterranean and Europe. The sea provided ready access to the land and people on the Iberian Peninsula, and invaders repeatedly arrived by the sea. But with its newfound independence and its monarch, perhaps Portugal's fortunes would change.

History had taught the Portuguese much about the sea's potential. The Phoenicians had taught them that natural resources could be taken from the lands around the seas. The Carthaginians had demonstrated how colonies could be formed for the benefit of the conqueror and how naval military power could hamper the growth efforts of competing countries. The Moors brought new technology, including the compass and astrolabe, which allowed the Portuguese to learn how to sail by the stars. With all of the hardships and challenges presented by the occupying powers, the Portuguese had also learned from these countries how to use the sea to their advantage. These lessons would prove to serve the new monarchy well.

Whereas northern and southern Portugal had been heavily populated, the central part of the country was nearly uninhabited after the Moors had been pushed out. At the same time, intermarriage had blended the Moors with the local populations in the south. Settlement of the country's middle section was encouraged, and many Christians and religious crusaders moved into the region. Various orders of the Catholic Church, such as the Benedictines, Franciscans, and Dominicans, also established themselves in the region. The difficult task of blending the cultures of the north and south also started during this era. Northerners had taken on many rough and arrogant attitudes after their successful efforts to drive out the Moors. At the same time, people in the south were more accepting and refined. With the differences, cultural conflicts became a problem. To address this issue, the Portuguese monarchy called upon religious military groups like the Knights Templar to maintain order. These crusaders would be given land in return for their efforts to maintain peace and political control.

Three social classes developed in early Portugal. The highest class was the clergy. They were the wealthiest, best educated,

After the Moors were expelled from Portugal in 1249, the Catholic Church became the primary religious institution in the country. Several Catholic orders, including the Benedictines, Franciscans, and Dominicans, established themselves in Portugal. Pictured here is Jerónimos Monastery, which is one of Lisbon's most famous landmarks.

and held the highest political offices after the king. The nobility was the second-highest class and had received most of its wealth from the king as a result of past support in pushing out the Moors. The nobility were owners of estates, and many of the larger landowners had their own private army. Knights would often serve the nobility. The serfs, or commoners, were the largest class and at the bottom of the pyramid in terms of power and influence.

By the late thirteenth century, land ownership issues served to divide the clergy from the king. King Denis (1279–1325) nationalized a number of the religious military sects. The largest of these was the Knights Templar, which was disbanded in 1312. Denis also prevented the Catholic Church from taking the wealth of this order and instead formed the Order of Our Lord Jesus Christ in 1318. This order was then given all of the wealth and possessions of the Knights Templar by Pope John XXII. King Denis also established the Crown as being independent from the papacy (rule of the pope) and declared that he was the supreme power in the country. As a result of this action and the seizing of assets, King Denis was thrown out of the circle of the Catholic Church. He later died in 1325 and was succeeded by Afonso IV (1325–1357).

It was during the reign of Afonso IV that another scourge came from the sea. This time it was not a human invader, but rather the bubonic plague, otherwise known as the dreaded "Black Death." This devastating disease first arrived in Portugal at ports and then spread into urban areas during the years 1348 and 1349. The disease killed more than one-third of the population and devastated many elements of society, not only in Portugal but also across Europe, the Middle East, and elsewhere in Asia.

The grandson of Afonso IV, Fernando I, did not have any male heirs—only a single daughter named Beatriz, who was married to the king of Castile, Juan I. When Fernando died in 1383, a power struggle followed. A man named João, Ferdinand's half brother, killed the chancellor of Fernando's widow, Leonor Teles. She then fled and asked Juan I to intervene with troops. The Castilian king responded and sent his army in 1384. Although faced with superior opposition, the Portuguese under João prevailed in the many years of war that followed, until peace was made with Castile in 1411. The peace followed a stunning Portuguese victory in the Battle of Aljubarrota. In this battle, a Portuguese army of only 7,000 defied all odds by quickly defeating an overwhelming force of 32,000 Castilian soldiers in only one-half hour.

AN ERA OF ADVENTURE, DISCOVERY, AND GREATNESS

Royal marriages during this era often were arranged to create political alliances. This was true in the case of Portugal. In 1387, King João married an English woman who was the daughter of royalty. Her name was Philippa of Lancaster. This marriage and the earlier support of the English against the Castilians cemented the start of a 500-year alliance between the English and Portuguese. Queen Philippa was a remarkable woman who instituted reforms in education and moral conduct. She also increased trade between Portugal and England. Philippa died of the plague at the age of 51 in 1415. Her marriage to King João had produced six extremely talented children. The most remarkable was Henrique, who is more commonly known as Prince Henry the Navigator. João and Philippa's oldest son, Duarte, succeeded João as king in 1433.

King João initiated the first efforts to extend Portugal's influence overseas. Duarte also followed this policy with mixed success. After a short reign, he died in 1438, at which time Afonso V came to the throne. While the throne changed hands, the maritime interests of Portugal were being led by Prince Henry, a visionary who initiated and organized the earliest European voyages of discovery. Henry was born in 1394 and his talents became obvious at a young age. In 1418, he established an innovative school for navigation, mapmaking, and shipbuilding at Sagres, which is located at the very tip of Cape Saint Vincent, the most southwestern point on the European mainland. Henry was not only a man of the sea, but was also deeply religious. He administered the Order of Christ and lived a strict personal life that reflected his faith.

The Order of Christ had numerous resources that Prince Henry was able to use in his maritime quests. Prince Henry's leadership resulted in a series of explorations and discoveries that would catapult Portugal to the status of a world power. Strangely, considering his impact, Henry himself never traveled by sea farther from home than across the Strait of Gibraltar. Sailors leaving from Sagres soon discovered the Madeira Islands and the Azores, both of which are autonomous regions of Portugal. This means that they are still tied to Portugal, but have local governance.

The exploration of other new lands followed, as Prince Henry and his subjects expanded their exploration southward along Africa's Atlantic coast. Slavery became a terrible by-product of the explorations of the 1440s, when the Portuguese began to recognize that huge profits could be made from capturing and selling slaves. The slave trade declined, though, when Prince Henry banned it in 1455.

Despite the fact that Prince Henry did not sail on the Portuguese voyages of discovery, he was the great mind behind the operation. He advanced maritime technology, obtained funding, and educated generations of Portuguese about the sea and sailing. Scholars and technicians at his school developed new ships, called caravels, and improved navigation and mapmaking. These sleek craft were faster and lighter than other ships of the day.

Truly, Henry the Navigator's mark on Portugal and the world has been lasting. He died in 1460, but Portuguese explorers carried on his legacy by seeking a water route to India and embarking on other voyages of discovery. Bartolomeu Dias

PRINCE HENRY
OF
PORTUGALL

CEUTA

Under the patronage and leadership of Prince Henry the Navigator, Portugal improved its sailing vessels and cartographic techniques, which went a long way in helping it to become the first European nation to explore West Africa. Henry is depicted here after the capture of the Moroccan city of Ceuta in 1415.

proved in 1488 that the Atlantic and Indian oceans were connected when he sailed around the southern tip of Africa. In 1497, Vasco da Gama was the first to travel by sea from Portugal to India. In 1500, Pedro Álvares Cabral set sail from Portugal for a second expedition to India. He ventured southwest and discovered Brazil, which he called Vera Cruz. He then continued his trip to India, but the discovery of Brazil was very important for both countries.

Having lived in Portugal from 1476 to 1484, Christopher Columbus was also a student of Portuguese maritime thinking. However, he was unable to secure funding for his expeditions from King João II and eventually had to go to Spain. There he obtained funding from Ferdinand and Isabella for his voyages westward across uncharted seas, which led to his "discovery" of the Americas. Magellan was another talented Portuguese mariner who could not get funding for his maritime endeavors. Thus, the Spanish funded his voyage, which became the first to circumnavigate the earth. (Although Magellan was killed in the Philippines in 1521 and therefore did not himself circle the globe.)

By the sixteenth century, Portuguese influence had spread to much of the world—coastal Africa, Madagascar, the Middle East, Mauritius, India (including Goa), Malaya, Indonesia, China (including Macau), and Brazil. At first the Portuguese were interested in discovery and commerce. This changed with their maritime achievements, and soon they found the benefits that colonies could present. In 1494, the world was literally divided by the Treaty of Tordesillas, or the Line of Demarcation. Pope Alexander VI arranged the treaty meeting, which arbitrarily divided the entire world (other than Europe) between Portugal and Spain. The line, which ultimately ran north to south roughly through the mouth of the Amazon River, gave Spain lands to the west and Portugal lands to the east. With the doors opened and sanctioned, the Portuguese colonization of Brazil began in the early sixteenth century. Colonization later followed in both Africa and Asia. Trading ports were established throughout the world in places like Malacca, Goa, Macau, and Nagasaki. By the second half of the sixteenth century, Portugal had established a vast empire and its royal family had become the richest in the world.

DECLINE OF THE PORTUGUESE EMPIRE

Portugal's expansionist efforts began to decline when, in 1557, Sebastião became the designated royal heir at the age of 14. Regents (appointed leaders who govern in the place of an actual monarch) ruled for him until 1568, when he assumed the title of king. His rule quickly led Portugal downward. In 1578, defying the advice of his commanders, he led an invasion of Morocco. His invasion failed miserably and Sebastião died in the battle for Alcázarquivir. This devastating defeat resulted in the death of 18,000 Portuguese soldiers, a loss that quickly opened the door for Spain to re-enter Portugal. Spain invaded in 1580 and Portugal was quickly defeated. Portugal was then annexed by Spain and ruled by the Spanish Habsburg kings for 60 years in the Iberian Union.

With Portugal under Spanish control in the Iberian Union, the empire began to disintegrate, especially in Asia. Opposition to Spanish rule turned into a successful rebellion in 1640. In 1641, the Portuguese returned a member of the House of Avis back to the throne and João IV became king of Portugal.

Brazil was one of the places where Portugal was successful in retaining its control. The Atlantic Ocean was the link between colony and colonizer and served as a water highway for activities between the two. Gold, diamonds, and Brazilwood were important resources found in Brazil that benefited Portugal. And tropical crops, such as coffee, cotton, and sugarcane, thrived in the moist tropical climate. Brazil remained under Portuguese control until 1822, when the Brazilians declared independence. However, Portuguese influence on Brazilian culture was significant. Religion, language, and music are just some of the many cultural traits that can be traced to Portugal. Brazil is the only country in the Americas where Portuguese is the official language.

As mentioned in Chapter 2, a violent and devastating earthquake shook Lisbon on All Saints' Day, November 1, 1755, destroying most of the city. The quake was just the beginning: a tsunami, ravaging fires, infections, disease, and famine followed over time, killing an estimated 100,000 people. Ultimately, the Portuguese pulled themselves from the rubble and ashes and began working to improve construction methods that would make the city less vulnerable to future earthquakes.

By the 1770s and 1780s, democratic revolutions were beginning to sweep across France and elsewhere in western Europe and in the United States. The Portuguese monarchy viewed these events with great concern, wary that the ideas of democracy might spread to the Iberian Peninsula. Royal families began to fear for their lives. To support other monarchies, Portuguese troops allied themselves with the English and were sent to fight against the French revolutionaries in Spain. With the rise of Napoleon in 1804, however, Portugal became neutral in the expanding conflict between France and England, though it continued to maintain close ties with the British. Portugal's neutrality did not stop Napoleon. He and Spain invaded Portugal in 1807 and seized Lisbon.

A later invasion attempt to further extend French influence was successfully repelled in 1810. During this invasion, the British and Portuguese armies simply wore out the French forces. Eventually the French had to withdraw because they were short of food and supplies. Although the Portuguese had finally prevailed, new ideas of constitutionalism and liberalism had entered Portuguese thinking. Thus, the fears of the royal family were about to be realized.

NEW THINKING, NEW CONSTITUTIONS, AND A DICTATORSHIP

The liberal thinking that had been introduced to Portugal while repelling Napoleon's forces had become a constant thorn in the side of the royal family. In 1822, João VI swore to uphold the new constitution, which created a constitutional monarchy.

However, political turmoil between the royalists (people supporting the royal family) and the liberals (those supporting democratic reforms) continued throughout the nineteenth century with the drafting of new constitutions, political battles, and insurrections.

Portugal fell into financial chaos at the end of the nineteenth century and declared bankruptcy in 1892. Carlos I had ascended to the throne in 1889 with the intent of recreating a Portuguese empire in Africa. This effort failed and by 1906, resistance to the monarch had increased due to corruption and governmental ineptitude. On February 1, 1908, King Carlos was riding in his carriage when he was attacked and killed by antiroyalists. His son, Manuel II, succeeded him on the throne and tried to revive the monarchy, but his efforts failed and the royal family sought refuge in England. Republicanism prevailed from 1910 until 1926, but Portugal's governments were like a revolving door—45 of them came and went during this 16-year period.

Portugal remained neutral for the first part of World War I but, with British prodding, finally joined the Allies in 1916. Inside the country, assassinations disrupted the Portuguese goverment: President Sidónio Pais was killed in 1918, and President António Machado Santos met the same fate three years later. Due to this continuing chaos, the military stepped in and overthrew the democratic government in 1926. This action paved the way for the rise of António de Oliveira Salazar, who eventually seized power and created a fascist dictatorship modeled after Benito Mussolini's regime in Italy. Salazar's fascist government stabilized the economy, but individual civil liberties were lost in the process. A heavy-handed police state with strict censorship followed. Salazar ruled for nearly 40 years until he was incapacitated by a stroke in 1968. He died two years later. A protégé of Salazar's, Marcelo Caetano, ruled until 1974, when a military coup forced him from power. It was not until 1976 that Portugal was able to again adopt a democratic constitution.

Portugal's tumultuous history has been greatly tied to the sea. The democratic era following 1976 has proven to be a period of political and economic advancement. These aspects will be discussed further in Chapters 5 and 6. But history has shown the ingenuity and strength of the Portuguese people and how they have blended the ideas of others with their own to create the society seen today. The Portuguese can carry their history with pride, because they have repeatedly shown their perseverance and character when faced with adversity and chaos.

4

People and Culture

Of all geographic information, perhaps nothing is more essential to understanding the geography of a place than its population and settlement (where people live). Certainly this holds true for Portugal. This chapter is divided into three primary sections. First, it investigates the demographic (statistical) aspects of the Portuguese population and explains the importance of these data. Second, it considers the various migrations that have affected the country's population through time. Finally, it explains the density and spatial distribution of Portuguese settlement.

POPULATION

Census data are often the first place geographers turn when trying to understand a land and its people. Few sources of information can tell one more about a country than its demographic data—statistical information pertaining to the human population. Numbers and density are important, as is an understanding of why people cluster in some areas and avoid others. But they do not tell the whole story. Such information as the rate of natural population increase, fertility rates, infant mortality rates, and life expectancy reveal a great deal about a country's development. So, too, do such figures as gross national product, the percentages of age groups within the population, and rural versus urban patterns of settlement. Migration trends and patterns also are extremely important, because they reveal human attitudes and levels of well-being in a location. This is just some of the demographic information that is readily available for all of the world's countries. Most of the data presented in this chapter have come from one of two sources: the *2006 World Population Data Sheet of the Population Reference Bureau* and the *CIA World Factbook: Portugal* (released in November 2006).

Once the foregoing facts are known, a geographer can begin answering other questions. For example, is the country's population too large or too small? Is it "overpopulated," or does it have too few resources and too poor an economy to adequately support its people? Is the population healthy and educated? Is the economy growing at a rate faster than that of the country's population? What can be learned from the country's in- or out-migration patterns? What impact does the country's economy (government, society, or natural environment) have on the population, people's well-being, and where people live? Answers to such questions are critical if one is to understand a country's geographic patterns and conditions.

Before continuing, a word of caution: Population figures often vary greatly from source to source. For example, "standard" sources place Portugal's population at between 9.9 and 10.9 million—a difference of one million, or roughly 10 percent. In this context, it is important to know that the last official census was taken in 2001, leaving five years (as this book is written) of guesswork. The situation is even more alarming in regard to urban populations. Again, "standard" sources give Lisbon's

Lisbon is Portugal's largest city and capital, with a metropolitan population of 2.7 million, or roughly 25 percent of the country's inhabitants. Pictured here is Rossio Square, or Pedro IV Square, which has been one of the city's primary gathering places since the Middle Ages.

population as being somewhere between 550,000 and nearly 2,500,000. This huge difference is easily explained: The low figure is for the main urban area, whereas the higher number refers to its metropolitan area (the city and all of its immediately surrounding communities). For most purposes, geographers really do not care about precise figures. Of much greater concern are general conditions and demographic trends—that is, are conditions good and getting better, bad and getting worse, or do they lie somewhere in between?

Demographic Data

Portugal's population (including the Azores and Madeira) is estimated to be 10.6 to 10.7 million (2006), which is relatively small in contrast to many other countries in western Europe or along the Mediterranean. The rate of natural population increase is a very low 0.1 percent per year, well below the annual world average of 1.2 percent rate of growth. In fact, the fertility rate (the average number of children born to each woman during her fertile years) is about 1.4 percent, well below the replacement level of 2.1 percent. If the current trend continues, the country's population—like that of many European countries—will decline unless dropping birthrates are balanced by in-migration. In fact, demographers project that Portugal's population will decline to 10.4 million by 2025 and drop further to 9.3 million by 2050. This would result in a whopping loss of about 1.3 million people, or 12 percent of the current population. As one might expect, the Portuguese government believes that population decline is a critical problem facing the country.

Most of Portugal's demographic data compare quite favorably with general patterns found throughout southern and western Europe. Infant mortality is quite low, at 3.8 deaths per 1,000 (versus 6.8 for the United States and 7.0 for all of Europe). Life expectancy is a very important index of human well-being; long lives usually suggest good health care, an educated populace, and a healthy economy. At birth, Portuguese people on average can expect to live 78 years—men, 74 years, and women, 81. These figures are almost identical to those of the United States, and are actually slightly higher than those for the entire European continent.

Interpreting the Data

Overall, the demographic data for Portugal show few causes for alarm. They reflect trends occurring today throughout much of Europe and elsewhere in the economically developed world. Certainly, there is nothing to suggest that a condition of "overpopulation" exists. The figures do, however, point to some possible future problems. For example, 17 percent of Portugal's population is 65 years of age or older, a situation quite common throughout most of Europe. That percentage, however, can be somewhat misleading. Portugal has had one of Europe's

Like many European countries, Portugal's population is aging: The population growth rate stands at just 0.36 percent a year, nearly all of which is the result of in-migration. Pictured here is former Portuguese president Mario Soares visiting women in an elderly people's home in Porto, Portugal, in 2006.

oldest populations for many decades because of very high rates of out-migration of young adults.

As a country's population ages, several problems can occur. Health-care costs escalate dramatically, as do other needs of the elderly. Social security can become a critical drain on a country's finances (a situation that the United States and many other developed countries face today). An aging population means a declining workforce, particularly at the lower end of the wage scale. There appear to be only two solutions to this problem. One is to increase the birthrate by offering incentives such as tax breaks, medical care, education benefits, and extended maternal leave with pay for new mothers. The other is to encourage in-migration. Through time, the single most significant factor explaining sharp changes in Portugal's population—whether decline, gain, or the male to female ratio—has been migration.

Family Planning

Despite the overwhelming dominance of Roman Catholicism and the Church's position against contraception, for several centuries Portugal has had one of Europe's lowest rates of population growth. Today the fertility rate (1.5 percent) is well below the replacement level, and the rate of natural increase (0.1 percent) is but a small fraction of the world average. Rather than being unique to Portugal, similar conditions exist throughout most of both Catholic and Protestant Europe. In Portugal's case, several factors can help explain low rate of growth.

First, as will be further discussed in the next section of this chapter, for much of the past half-millennium, millions of Portuguese have left their country. Out-migration has long been a safety valve to relieve population pressures at home. Many Portuguese left for the country's various colonies. Others left the country in search of better economic opportunities in North America or elsewhere in western Europe. Typically it was males who migrated, resulting in Portugal being left with many more women than men. The imbalance resulted in many single women and women who delayed starting a family because they were separated from their husbands. More recently, the country's population has aged, leaving many people beyond the years during which they want (or are able to bear) children. Finally, as is true throughout the developed world, improved living standards almost always result in lower fertility rates.

As a population becomes more educated and more affluent, families generally want fewer children. When the status of women improves and as more women choose to enter the workforce, fertility rates also drop. All of these changes are the result of a major shift in both settlement and culture. To most rural people who practice a traditional folk (self-sufficient) culture, children represent capital, or wealth. They can help the family gather firewood, fetch water, herd livestock, work in the home garden, and perform other helpful tasks. In a contemporary urban society, however, children are a financial drain because there is little they can do to contribute economically. Therefore, worldwide, urban families tend to have fewer children than do their rural counterparts. Such declines in a country's birthrate, of course, generally result from deliberate family planning and decisions.

PEOPLE ON THE MOVE

Migration is a generic term used in reference to the relocation of people who move from place to place, generally across a political border. (If a person relocates to another community within his own state, though, he, or she, would move, rather than migrate.) A person leaving a country is an *emigrant;* one entering a country to establish residence is an *immigrant.* Population geographers have long recognized that the primary reason people move is to improve their economic well-being. Marriage, for example, is considered by social scientists to be an economic arrangement in which the husband generally is responsible for the wife and children. Students go off to college in the belief that their education will better prepare them to compete for good jobs, which will lead to a comfortable standard of living. Throughout the world, people flock to jobs. Basically, no matter where they are in the world, most people move in the direction of what they hope will be better economic conditions.

Emigration and immigration do not occur randomly; few people move without a good reason. Rather, migration patterns are the result of an often-complex combination of "push-and-pull" factors. Push factors are those that influence people to leave an area, such as few or poorly paying jobs. Pull factors are those conditions that attract people to a location. Again, better economic opportunity is the primary magnet that attracts immigrants.

Out-migration

Portugal has experienced several "waves" of out-migration that occurred at different times and often for different reasons. Beginning in the fifteenth century and continuing well into the twentieth century, many Portuguese moved to the country's present or past colonies. Widespread colonization and settlement followed on the heels of early exploration. Trading posts were established that offered opportunities in trade and management, and administrators were needed to oversee Portugal's political interests in their newly acquired territories. Some migrants went to colonies in Africa, such as Angola or Mozambique; others went to various Asian possessions. Most, however, immigrated to Brazil, which occupies nearly one-half of the South American continent and was once a Portuguese possession.

Beginning in the mid-1800s and continuing into the latter part of the twentieth century, Portugal experienced massive out-migration. During that period, more than 2.5 million Portuguese left the country. In western Europe, only Ireland lost more of its people. Portugal, in many respects, was the least-developed country in all of western Europe. It was poorly governed, the economy was stagnant, there were few jobs, and land was scarce. People held little hope for achieving a better life at home. During this period, Brazil and the United States were the most popular destinations. Approximately half of all immigrants went to the United States, and today about 3.5 million people in the Americas claim Portuguese ancestry. Another

30 percent went to Brazil, where some one million Portuguese were living toward the end of the twentieth century.

During the 1960s and 1970s, the population fell by about 300,000 people. At that time, however, an estimated 80 percent of those people immigrated to European countries, many illegally. France and (at the time) West Germany were the preferred destinations. In fact, according to one estimate, 8 percent of Portugal's population lived in France. These were difficult times for the Portuguese. Their country was fighting to retain its African colonies, and many males left to avoid military service. In 1974, Portugal was locked in a political revolution and the economy was in shambles.

The situation began to improve during the 1980s. Democratic reforms introduced during the mid-1970s were beginning to stabilize the country politically. In 1984, Portugal was admitted to what is now the European Union (EU). This resulted in a huge spurt of economic development and growth that continues today. For the first time in memory, Portuguese could stay within their country and make a decent living.

Immigration

If the prospect of economic gain is the chief pull factor in migration, until very recent times, Portugal had little if anything to offer to immigrants. However, during the past three or four decades, conditions have undergone a remarkable change. The tide turned in the 1970s. Portugal lost its African colonies, resulting in a flood of political refugees and Portuguese who simply wanted to return home. Some estimates place the number of immigrants who have left former colonies as high as 800,000. At the time, this would have amounted to approximately 10 percent of the Portuguese population.

Today, immigration is the primary contributor to Portugal's population growth. Most immigrants are Portuguese returning to their homeland, either in the ancestral sense or

Over the last 30 years, most of Portugal's population growth rate has been due to in-migration from residents of the country's former African colonies, including the tiny West African nation of Guinea-Bissau. Pictured here are Portuguese and Guinea-Bissau refugees who have arrived in Lisbon after a coup deposed President João Bernardo Vieira in 1998.

by birth. Some, of course, are internationals from former colonies. With its newfound economic prosperity, the country is even beginning to attract migrants from poor regions of eastern Europe.

SETTLEMENT

Settlement—the distribution of people across an area—reveals a good deal in terms of geography. What is the population density within a country? Does the figure suggest a condition of over-crowding and perhaps even overpopulation? Where do the people live and why? Is the population primarily rural or urban, and what are the trends and significance of these patterns? Is settlement clustered or scattered about the land? How are concentrations of people explained and why do people avoid some places? These are just some of the questions related to Portuguese settlement.

Population Density

Portugal has a population density of about 300 people per square mile (116 per square kilometer). Such figures are all but mean-ingless, however, unless they are placed in a geographical con-text. After all, some of the world's richest and poorest countries both have very high population densities; the same can be said for countries with very low densities. Portugal's density is more than three times that of the United States, but is comparable to most other European countries and lower than some. What is important is not the density of people; rather, it is the ability of a country to support its population. In other words, four decades ago the country's population density was considerably lower than today. But its economy was unable to provide adequately for the people. A condition of severe overpopulation existed and millions of people left the country in the hope of finding a bet-ter life. Today, although the country has many more people and a much higher population density, its economy is prospering, as are most of its people. Few modern observers would suggest that Portugal is overpopulated.

Rural vs. Urban Settlement

With an almost even split between rural settlement (47 percent) and urban (53 percent), Portugal remains one of Europe's most rural countries. The continent as a whole is

Approximately 47 percent of Portugal's population lives in rural areas, most of whom are farmers. Small villages such as Povoa Dao, in northern Portugal, are becoming increasingly rare as more and more Portuguese move into urban areas.

75 percent urbanized, and in some countries (such as Germany, Italy, and Belgium), about 90 percent of all people live in cities. Most rural people are farmers, many of whom are peasants raising crops for their own subsistence and continuing to practice traditional folkways. Only gradually are many of them—particularly those living in more remote areas—being integrated into the country's cash-based and increasingly industrial and service-oriented economy.

The Portuguese government classifies about 150 urban centers as being cities, a designation based on such factors as population, infrastructure, services, and other conditions. Most of the cities are rather small. In fact, only six urban centers have a population that exceeds 100,000. The following figures are based on 2002 data and are for the main city area, rather than its metropolitan area: Lisbon (558,100), Porto (263,600), Amadora (175,200), Braga (114,300), Setúbal (113,800), and Coimbra (102,900).

Of these cities, Lisbon and Porto clearly stand above the others in size. In fact, metropolitan Lisbon, with a population estimated to be as high as 2.7 million, is home to 1 of every 4 Portuguese. Located in southern Portugal's Estremadura region, the city just keeps growing. Lisbon is what geographers call a *primate city*, one that towers above all others in importance. It is the country's population, political, economic, and social center. Actually, Amadora, the country's third-largest urban area, is for all practical purposes a Lisbon suburb, because it is only a few miles away. Phoenician traders first settled Lisbon around 1200 B.C. and some settlement has occupied its current site since that time. Much of Lisbon's growth can be traced to its location on a fertile alluvial (river-deposited silt) plain, at the mouth of the Tagus River, and on what many call Europe's best natural harbor.

Porto is the country's second-largest city, with some 1.3 million people living in its metropolitan area. It is located in northern Portugal's Minho Province, near the mouth of the Douro River, where it was founded during the fourth century A.D. The city's name suggests its early (and continuing) function: an important port (*porto* means "port" in Portuguese). The city is world famous for port wine, which is produced from grapes grown within the region.

Braga (Minho Province, north of Porto), Setúbal (south of Lisbon, in Estremadura Province), and Coimbra (on the Mondégo River, situated roughly halfway between Lisbon and Porto) are important regional economic centers.

POPULATION DISTRIBUTION

Portugal's population is not evenly distributed throughout the country. The lowest densities are found in those provinces that border Spain and throughout the southern half of the country, east and south of Lisbon. Physical environmental conditions can help explain the lower density in these regions. Much of eastern Portugal is rugged, with few areas suited to farming. Southern Portugal experiences a Mediterranean subtropical climate that receives less precipitation than in the north and also is subject to severe summer drought. Culturally and historically, the Portuguese have always been a coastal people who look seaward, rather than landward. This factor helps explain the coastal orientation of the country's population.

The main areas having the highest populations are the more humid northern half of the country and fertile river valleys and coastal plains. In the latter locations, water-deposited alluvial soils tend to be quite fertile and make productive agriculture possible.

This chapter has focused upon Portugal's population and settlement. But it has revealed very little about the well-being of the Portuguese people. The next two chapters will take an in-depth look at Portugal's government and economy. These chapters will discuss why the country's population is now beginning to grow and how its standard of living is experiencing remarkable development.

5

Government and Politics

Portugal's political past has been colored by a variety of types of government. These have included a monarchy, constitutional monarchy, republic, dictatorship, and rule by an array of foreigners who swept into the country. Relative to other western European countries, democracy was very late in coming to Portugal. This factor greatly hindered the country's economic and social development. Fortunately, once democracy took root, the country has taken a much more positive turn.

Today Portugal is a modern parliamentary democracy. In 1976, it adopted its current constitution. *Democracy* is a term derived from the Greek word *demos,* which means "the common people." Another Greek word, *kratein,* means "to rule." Thus *demos kratein* becomes *democracy*, which means the "common people rule."

Portugal's 1976 constitution started what many have called Portugal's Second Republic, with the first having begun in the early twentieth century. The constitution has been amended (changed) many times, but serves as the highest law in the country. An early challenge to the country was that there were a number of strong political parties in the late 1970s. These included larger political parties such as the Popular Democratic Party, Portuguese Communist Party, Socialist Party, Portuguese Democratic Movement, and the Social Democratic Central Party. Other minor parties also were active and represented in the political process. A political structure with many political parties is called a multiparty system. Today, Portugal continues to have this type of system, whereas places like the United States have what is referred to as a two-party system.

The problem presented by having many political parties is that it is difficult to form and keep governments. Political parties must form coalitions with each other to secure a majority within a governing body. Having a majority allows a coalition to select the prime minister and rule the country. Historically, however, with so many parties in Portugal, alliances were often fragile and governments were sometimes quickly replaced. One coalition government in 1978 lasted only 17 days. Today, there are still many political parties, but only two received more than 8 percent of the vote in the 2005 Parliamentary elections. The largest, the Portuguese Socialist Party, garnered more than 45 percent of the vote and won 121 of 230 seats in the one-house Parliament, called the Assembly of the Republic. By having only a one-house legislative branch, Portugal (like the state of Nebraska's legislature) has what is called a unicameral Parliament.

The second-strongest party in the 2005 elections was the Social Democratic Party, which gained 75 seats in the Assembly of the Republic. Three other parties received the remaining 34 seats in Parliament and another five political parties gained no seats. Thus, although officially having a multiparty system, the Portuguese Socialist Party and the Social Democratic Party have become dominant in recent years.

The Assembly of the Republic, or Palácio de São Bento, is the home of Portugal's Parliament. Originally constructed as a Benedictine monastery in 1598, the building has served as the home of Parliament since 1834.

Lisbon, Portugal's largest city, is the nation's capital. The city has a natural beauty with its picturesque, hilly location on the Tagus River. In addition to the government buildings, there are many national museums such as the Maritime Museum, Military Museum, Museum of Water, Museum of Ancient Art, and the fantastic carriage displays at the world famous Coach Museum. There are numerous other museums in the city that record the country's past, including a tile museum. Lisbon has served as the capital of Portugal since A.D. 1147, when the Moors were finally driven out of the country. The Assembly of the Republic resides in a gorgeous neoclassical (new form of an old style) monastery that dates to the sixteenth century. It was damaged in the earthquake of 1755 and by fire in 1895, but was repaired and finally refurbished to serve as the Parliament Building in the 1940s.

The foundation of the country's political structure is based on the 1976 constitution, which has frequently been amended. The seventh revision of the constitution was made in 2005. In this document, the branches of government are named and responsibilities are outlined. Also defined in the constitution are the rights of citizens, along with other fundamental processes and practices for governing the country.

THE THREE BRANCHES OF GOVERNMENT

Portugal's constitution identifies the three branches of government: the legislative, executive, and judicial. The executive branch is responsible for enforcing the laws of the country. Portugal's executive branch is headed by a president who serves as chief of state. The president is chosen in a nationwide election and can serve up to two five-year terms. The president can make and dissolve sessions of the assembly and serves as the commander in chief of the country's armed forces. As the chief executive, the president also enforces laws and appoints people to key political positions. A veto allows the president to reject legislation from the assembly, but in reality the veto can be overridden with a simple majority vote, and so this power is not very useful.

The prime minister heads the national government of Portugal and is responsible for managing the day-to-day work of the government. To carry out this role, the prime minister appoints a cabinet called the Council of Ministers, which includes members of various government offices designed to oversee specific functions. The council normally includes 15 to 18 members who hold such offices as the minister of Finance, Justice, Economic Affairs, Education, Internal Affairs, Environment, and Culture. Most of the ministers are members of the assembly, but this is not a requirement. These ministerial offices create government policies and have the responsibility of implementing laws and policies.

The prime minister is usually the leader of the majority political party, or the ruling coalition of parties. Individuals holding this office may serve up to four years. They can serve for a shorter period of time if the government is dissolved or if a ruling coalition falls apart. The prime minister can also call for early elections. This is sometimes done when the prime minister's party has garnered a good deal of support. Elections will be called in the belief that the party can gain, or at least maintain, seats in the Assembly of the Republic.

The Assembly of the Republic is the legislative branch of the government, which means it has the responsibility of making public policy for Portugal. The assembly consists of 230 members, called deputies, who are elected to four-year (or shorter) terms. Anyone older than 18 years can be a candidate for a seat in the assembly. Political parties submit lists of candidates, and seats in the assembly are proportionally divided out to parties. Thus, deputies represent the entire country and not just one region.

The primary function of the assembly is to create laws for the country. The body can also amend the constitution by passing constitutional laws, a move that requires a two-thirds vote by members. Much of the work of the assembly is done in committees. Some of these groups have a specific short-term task, while others are standing committees that continue session after session.

The judiciary is the third branch of government and is responsible for administering justice in Portugal and interpreting the country's laws. The courts are independent and the Supreme Court of Justice is designated as the highest court in the country. Judges are appointed. The constitutional court has strong powers in that it can decide whether laws passed by the assembly are constitutional or not. The influence of Roman law and the French legal system have played a large role in Portugal's legal and judicial structure.

POLITICAL SUBDIVISIONS

Portugal, like most countries, is divided into geographic regions that serve as political subdivisions. In 2007, the country was divided into 18 districts and the two autonomous (self-governing) regions of the Azores and Madeira. However, a transition was taking place in the early twenty-first century, when new subdivision designations were created and called administrative regions, municipalities, and civil parishes. Local governments in Portugal are responsible for public policy efforts in their own area of jurisdiction. These responsibilities include such issues as education, public health, local development, public safety, and cultural and sporting facilities. Local governments work with such matters as schools, streets, local law enforcement, and fire protection.

Local governments in Portugal typically have two branches. One provides for the management of local government and enforcement of laws. The second provides for policy formation and local legislative functions. For example, parishes have a parish authority who serves as the executive, and a parish assembly conducts the legislative functions. The composition of municipalities and administrative regions is the same; they also have assemblies for legislative actions and an authority who operates as the executive.

RIGHTS OF CITIZENS

Citizens are the foundation of any democracy. In their contract with the government, which is found in the constitution, citizens have various protected rights. Portugal, as a modern democracy with a fairly new constitution, has protected its citizens in a number of key areas. Some of the key protections and liberties guaranteed to citizens by the constitution include:

- Equality under the law with respect to sex, race, language, religion, education, sexual orientation, and other factors.

- Guaranteed access to the law and courts.

- The right to resist any order that infringes upon the rights, freedoms, or guarantees to citizens.

- The right to life. (Portugal's constitution outlaws the death penalty.)

- The right to freedom and security.

- The right to have legal counsel and the guarantee of being innocent until proven guilty.

- The right to privacy.

- The right to access all computer information that concerns the individual citizen.

- Freedom of expression.

- Freedom of the press.

- Freedom of conscience, religion, and worship.

- Freedom to teach and learn.

- The right to travel and emigrate (freedom of movement).

- Freedom of association and the right to meet and demonstrate.

- Freedom to choose a profession and the right to work.

- The right to vote and run for office.

- The right to own private property.

- The right to health care (Portugal provides its citizens with health care.)

- The right to education and culture.

Portugal's protections include a mix of traditional freedoms and rights, but also newer issues like the right to access computer information about themselves and government-provided health care. The constitution is consistent with the protections provided by the United Nations Declaration of Human Rights. (Portugal has been a member of the organization since 1955.) A citizen's only duty identified in the constitution is to defend the nation.

FOREIGN RELATIONS

Portugal has been involved in foreign affairs for centuries. As a former colonial power, it is no surprise that the country is still active today in the international community. The country belongs to a number of international organizations, including the United Nations, European Union, Council of Europe, NATO, UNESCO, World Trade Organization, World Health Organization, and more than 60 other bodies. Portugal's international involvement greatly increased after its dictatorship ended and it became a democracy.

Perhaps the most important political tie has been Portugal's inclusion in the European Union (EU). This body has changed the political face of Europe by adding a multinational political structure that supercedes that of the individual nation. Portugal joined the European Union in 1986. The EU has a European Parliament of 732 members. Portugal is represented by 24 members, who are elected by Portuguese citizens. Members of the European Parliament (MEP) are elected for five-year terms. Members do not sit by country, but rather by political parties or affiliations. Parliament strives to promote political and economic integration while respecting the nationalities and cultures of the member countries. Thus, laws passed are often designed to promote consistency between the laws of EU members.

As a founding member of NATO, Portugal has been involved in a number of peacekeeping efforts. Portuguese troops served in NATO actions in Bosnia-Herzegovina, Kosovo, and Afghanistan during the 1990s and early years of the twenty-first century.

The country also has been active in its agreement to uphold international treaties. Some of these are for environmental protection, such as the agreements on biodiversity, climate change, air pollution, ozone layer protection, endangered species, and desertification. Others relate to a wide range of international interests, including the law of the sea, open skies for airlines, prohibition of biological and toxic weapons, and a treaty for the suppression of terrorist bombings. The range of international agreements is truly extensive, and Portugal has been deeply involved in most of these activities.

To conduct the daily affairs between Portugal and other countries, there is an extensive network of embassies and consulates around the world. The president appoints ambassadors, while the Ministry of Foreign Affairs is responsible for the day-to-day matters related to foreign affairs.

The Community of Portuguese Language Countries (CPLC) is a special organization that consists of Portugal and seven former colonies: Brazil, Angola, Cape Verde, East Timor, Guinea-Bissau, Mozambique, and São Tome and Príncipe. This political and diplomatic organization has the primary goal of promoting the Portuguese language. It also has helped during times of strife in member states, such as when coups (overthrow of governments) in Guinea-Bissau and São Tome and Príncipe were resolved.

Perhaps the most significant, long-term foreign relationship of Portugal has been with the United Kingdom. The two countries have been linked under the Treaty of Alliance since 1373. This relationship was further cemented in the Treaty of Windsor in 1386 and through a number of marriages between royal family members from the two countries. Today, this partnership continues with frequent state visits and numerous political and economic activities taking place between the two nations.

Another important foreign relationship continues to be with Spain. Sharing the Iberian Peninsula, both their cultures

Portugal and Spain share a common history and heritage and continue to maintain a strong diplomatic relationship. Pictured here are Portuguese president Anibal Cavaco Silva (second from left) and his wife, Maria (left), with King Juan Carlos I and Queen Sofia of Spain during Silva's first trip abroad after becoming president in January 2006.

and history have been and continue to be closely linked. Today they are key trading partners and are joined in a number of other ways. One ongoing conflict between the two countries is that Portugal does not recognize Spain's claim to the territory of Olivença, a city that borders the two nations but is presently administered by Spain. The two countries have different interpretations about treaties signed in 1801 and 1815 that have bred disagreement. Portugal contends that the city should be returned to its rule according to provisions in the two treaties. Fortunately, this situation has not impeded the good relations between the neighbors.

After centuries of conflict, invasion, foreign rule, monarchies, and dictatorships, Portugal has become an effective democracy. Citizens have used their newfound freedoms to the benefit of the country. As a stable country and now a member of the European Union, Portugal has made many advances during recent decades and looks to the remainder of the twenty-first century with optimism. Instead of being a remote outpost on the western, far edge of the continent, Portugal is today poised for new possibilities as a core member of a new Europe.

CHAPTER

6

Portugal's Economy

A country's economy is much like the engine in a car. Vital elements are necessary to make it work, including fuel, oxygen, and a spark to trigger the engine's combustion. Economies also need key elements to feed, clothe, provide housing, educate, and defend a society. Economic production of goods and services is the outcome of an economy, while a car produces movement from one location to another. The government operates much like oxygen as it can either stifle or support economic development. Land, labor, and capital supply the fuel for an economy. At the same time, effective management provides the spark of ingenuity and the plans for consistency in production or in providing services. As is true with a car, the necessary elements in an economy can operate efficiently, or they may occasionally need a tune-up or repairs.

Effective economies provide their citizens with a quality of lifestyle that includes such things as health care, education, public services, low unemployment, law enforcement, and adequate food, clothing, and shelter. People with well-paying jobs can provide for themselves, while others may need assistance provided by charity or from the government. Portugal is a modern economy that has gradually entered the larger community of the European Union. Still, the country has a multi-faceted economy that provides a wide range of activities. Among these are communication and transportation systems, the exploitation of natural resources, manufacturing, fishing, tourism, agriculture, and many other resources. This chapter investigates how the Portuguese economy works and the important elements that make it work. It also examines the impact that the economy has in providing the basis for the survival and prosperity of its citizens.

Since entering the European Union (EU) in 1986, Portugal has developed a diversified economy and, since the beginning of 2002, has used the euro as its currency. Before 2002, the Portuguese currency was called the *escudo*, which means "shield."

The service industry in Portugal has greatly expanded in recent years. Most of these advances have been in the financial, retail, and telecommunications sectors. Today, services make up 60 percent of the jobs in the labor force, which compares to 68 percent in Canada and 79 percent in the United States. Industrial work in Portugal makes up another 30 percent of the jobs for the labor force. The agricultural sector trails at a distant 10 percent of the population, although many people continue to be engaged in farming. Because much of the agriculture is at a subsistence level, this activity produces only about 5 percent of the country's gross domestic product (GDP). The fact that the number of people engaged in farming is double that of their productivity suggests that Portuguese agriculture is relatively inefficient.

Although Portugal's economy has become diversified since it joined the European Union in 1986, the country is still a major producer of corks for bottled wine. Pictured here are cork inspectors at the A. Silva Company in Porto, Portugal, which produces approximately one million corks a day.

Portugal has some inherent economic advantages in that labor costs are lower than in most other countries in the EU. For example, in 2001, Portugal's average hourly wage was 7 euros, whereas the average for the EU was 21.4 euros per hour. The cheaper labor costs have helped the country attract foreign investments, but this advantage may be changing. Many countries in eastern Europe are now joining the EU. These countries also have lower wages and have the advantage of being closer to big European markets such as Germany and Italy. Thus, the Portuguese advantage of low labor costs may diminish with increased competition from countries such as Hungary, Romania, Poland, and others.

Keeping Portugal's economic engine running efficiently is a key responsibility of the government. Next, the major aspects of the Portuguese economy will be explored to gain a better understanding of how their economic machine keeps running and is getting stronger.

AGRICULTURE: THE TRADITIONAL ECONOMY

Agriculture has been important to Portugal for centuries. It is a key part of the folk culture that is still practiced in much of rural Portugal. It is also a necessity of life for people to have food. As societies advance, fewer and fewer workers are needed to produce food to feed a country because of improvements in agricultural technology. Today, 10 percent of Portugal's population is still engaged in agriculture. This compares with only 1 percent in the United States, about 2 percent in Canada, and slightly under 1 percent in Germany. Each of these three countries (and many others) has much lower percentages of the population engaged in agriculture than does Portugal. This means that they are more efficient, because production per farmer is much higher due to modern equipment, better seeds, and the widespread use of fertilizers, pesticides, and weed-killing chemicals. Portugal's inefficiency is further demonstrated by the fact that the country today imports more food than it exports.

Some of the agricultural products grown in Portugal include wheat, maize, rice, potatoes, olives, barley, oilseed, tobacco, fruits, vegetables, and cork. The country also produces a variety of livestock, including cattle, sheep, goats, pigs, and poultry. This production is smaller due to the limited pasture-lands. There is also a small dairy industry.

Portugal is also a large producer of grapes that are often used in making wines. Romans introduced winemaking to Portugal more than a thousand years ago, and the industry has prospered ever since. A regional type of wine called port is named after the city of Porto, where wineries use grapes from the Douro River valley region. Today, the country ranks near the top 10 in production of wine, and there are many vineyards

Portugal ranks among the top 10 countries in the world in wine production. One of the primary wine producing regions is northern Portugal's Douro River valley, which is renowned for its production of port wine. Pictured here is a worker carrying a basket full of grapes near the town of Vila Real.

scattered across the country. In addition, the country supplies about half of the world's cork wood—thus, Portugal is the predominant supplier of wine cork in the world. Other primary, or extractive, industries include forest products and fisheries.

MANUFACTURING INDUSTRY

Manufacturing is an important sector in Portugal's economy, producing more than 27 percent of the country's GDP. Most of the manufacturing is located in or near Lisbon and other nearby cities such as Setúbal. Smaller centers of manufacturing cluster around the northern cities of Porto, Braga, and Aveiro.

A wide variety of goods and products are manufactured in Portugal. Important processing industries include wood pulp and products, paper, oil refining, fish, and cement. Other basic industries manufacture textiles, footwear, chemicals, steel, ceramics, rubber and plastic products, and metalworks. There are also production plants that produce electronics of various types, including communications equipment, rail transportation equipment, aerospace equipment, ship construction and refurbishment, and cars. Some of these industries are owned by Portuguese interests, but foreign investment and ownership has also proceeded at a rapid pace in the industrial sector of the economy. Volkswagen, Accor (hotels), and Siemens (technology) are just three examples of foreign companies that have invested in Portugal.

COMMUNICATION AND TRANSPORTATION

All contemporary forms of communication and transportation are found in Portugal today. These two systems are vitally important because they move people or information and connect people and places. Communication comes in many forms, including mass media such as newspapers, magazines, radio, and television. More personal forms like telephones, mail systems, and e-mail are used to connect individuals. Transportation systems move goods and people from one location to another. Forms of transportation range from jets to subways. Today, Portugal has access to the world's most modern and efficient types of communication and transportation systems.

As of 2006, Portugal had 219 FM and AM radio stations and 62 domestic television stations. These are supplemented by hundreds of channels now available from satellites and cable systems that carry programs from around the world. Local newspapers are published from the Azores to the Spanish border, with 10 published in Lisbon alone. Special publications also exist. For example, there are two publications dedicated exclusively to football (soccer), named *A Bola* and *Record*, which have a distribution of more than 100,000. This circulation is as large as that of the major newspapers in Portugal.

The country has more than 4 million land phone lines and a whopping 11.5 million cell phones—more than one cell phone for every man, woman, and child in the country. Nearly 8 million Portuguese use the Internet and .pt is the country code for Portugal.

Transportation systems include roads, rail, water, air, and pipelines that are used to move oil and gas. The country has 48,759 miles (78,470 kilometers) of roads and 1,771 miles (2,850 kilometers) of railroad tracks. The Douro River is also a major water transportation site with 130 miles (210 kilometers) of water being navigable upstream from the city of Porto. Portugal has 66 airports, with Lisbon serving as the country's major air hub for both domestic and international passengers and cargo traffic.

The sea continues to serve as another major transportation route for Portugal. With a large merchant marine fleet, much of the country's trade passes through Lisbon or one of the other major ports in Leixoes, Setúbal, or Sines. Most of the ships carry cargo, but passenger cruise ships also make frequent stops in Lisbon.

ECONOMIC RESOURCE DEVELOPMENT

Portugal has the sea as a natural economic resource, but other natural elements significantly contribute to the economy. The country's limited mineral deposits have not been widely developed until recent decades. A rich copper and tin deposit was discovered in 1977 at Neves-Corvo. This site has greatly helped the country develop its mining industry. Now the country is one of the largest producers of copper in the EU. Other natural resources mined in Portugal include tungsten, iron ore, uranium, gypsum, salt, marble, slate, granite, gold, and silver.

Unfortunately, the country lacks significant deposits of key energy producing fossil fuels—coal, petroleum, and natural gas. As a result, Portugal must import much of its energy from other countries. Russia supplies much of the natural gas used in the country, while Norway has become another provider during the first decade of the twenty-first century. Despite the lack of fossil fuels, Portugal is able to provide at least some of its own energy needs. A major natural resource is the country's amazing rivers. These waterways supply the country with hydroelectric power that is safe and clean. More than 1,000 dams and reservoirs harness the hydroelectric potential of Portugal's many rivers. The Alentejo Dam, located on the Guadiana River, was built in 1998 and flooded in 2002. Much of the river is on the border between Spain and Portugal, about 10 miles (16 kilometers) north of the town of Moura. The dam's immense reservoir is now the largest artificial lake in all of Europe.

Today, dams are found on nearly all of the country's rivers. Efforts to develop dams and reservoirs on the country's remaining waterways, such as the Sabor River, are often met with strong resistance. This resistance is due to the fact that there can be major tradeoffs when dams are constructed, and a country must examine both the costs and benefits of new dams. In the case of the Sabor, it is one of the last remaining wild rivers in Portugal. If a dam is built, farmland will be flooded by the new reservoir, and wildlife habitats will be lost. Other dam reservoirs have buried ancient rock art drawings below the waters. Thus, there are both great advantages and disadvantages to Portuguese dam construction, and the battle over the Sabor River continues today.

Even though Portugal produces a good deal of hydroelectric power, the country still needs to import energy from other countries because of the lack of gas and coal. This shortage has caused the country to become more creative in energy generation. Other natural energies now being explored include the sun, wind, and even waves. For example, a major funding of wind-generated electricity was initiated in 2006 with a goal of building 48 wind farms. Solar energy also is being harnessed by a facility located on the southeast coast.

In a new development, wave power farms are being used on an experimental basis in northern Portugal. A site three miles off the coast near Aguadoura, Póvoa de Varzim is where the trial generators began to be placed in 2006. The generators look like giant, floating sausages that measure nearly 400 feet (120 meters) long and 11 feet (3.5 meters) wide. Each unit is nearly 100 feet (30 meters) longer than an American football field and 1.5 feet (.5 meters) wider than the height of a standard basketball hoop. The Portuguese, once again blessed by the seas, believe that wave power will eventually generate 20 percent of the country's electricity needs. This effort will make Portugal far less dependent on other countries for energy and may eventually help it become an energy exporter.

The land has also blessed Portugal with excellent sea access and natural ports. The Port of Lisbon on the Tagus River is the country's leading harbor. It has a natural deep-water harbor that has been used for a thousand years. There, a visitor will find tankers, container ships, and cruise vessels that connect the capital with the world. The port is well connected to other transportation systems, including railroads and highways, which allow products to move easily to and from the port. Warehouses surround the port, and companies use these facilities to store arriving and departing goods.

The port at Leixoes serves the city of Porto and the interior of the north. One-fourth of the country's trade goes through the Leixoes facility. With an extensive coastline, Portugal has a number of natural harbors, but the ports at Lisbon and Leixoes are the most developed, with other major activities also taking place in Setúbal and Sines.

TOURISM

Each year, hundreds of thousands of tourists flock to Portugal. They go to enjoy the sunny beaches, historical sites, landscape, religious sites, and the warm and enchanting hospitality of the Portuguese people. Tourist treasures such as Lisbon, the Douro River, Sintra, Estoril, Fátima, glorious beaches,

Thousands of tourists travel to Portugal each year to relax on the country's beautiful beaches. One of the most popular destinations is the Algarve Coast, which is located on the southern tip of Portugal and known for its warm Mediterranean climate and inexpensiveness.

medieval castles, and picturesque craggy cliffs and vistas all serve as sites that entice visitors. Prices are also lower than in most of western Europe. Most tourists come from Europe, primarily Spain, but increasingly the world is discovering the allure of Portugal. The number and variety of attractions are immense and serve to make tourism a very key element in the country's economy.

Tourists contribute to Portugal's economy in that they require transportation, guides, places to stay, meals, and other travelers' needs. Many attractions also have entry fees to the site and the services it provides. All of these activities create service jobs. Tourism is considered to be environmentally friendly and it assists in the country's balance of trade with other nations. Tourism generates about 5 percent of the country's GDP, with that amount increasing significantly each year.

FOREIGN TRADE AND THE EUROPEAN UNION

Portugal joined the European Community (now the European Union, or EU) in 1986. In 2007, there were 27 independent member states, which made the EU the largest confederation in the world. The EU works in a variety of ways to improve the region's trade, agriculture, taxation, energy, and monetary policy. Other issues of concern to the European Union include human rights, education, public health, culture, and food safety. The euro, adopted by Portugal in 2002, is now the common monetary system of the EU and it has quickly become a leading currency in world markets.

As a member of the European Union, Portugal has benefited from the relationships provided by the confederation. Foreign investment has increased and labor, goods, and services now move more efficiently between member countries. Most of Portugal's key trading partners are members of the EU. Key trading partners and the approximate percentage of Portugal's exports that they receive include: Spain (26 percent), France (13 percent), Germany (12 percent), United Kingdom (8 percent), and Italy (4 percent). The other important country for exports, outside of the EU, is the United States with 5.4 percent. A surprising fact is that none of Portugal's top six export trading partners is a former colony (such as Brazil or Angola).

Imported goods coming into Portugal also reflect the ties to EU members. Leading sources of imported goods are Spain (29 percent), Germany (13 percent), France (9 percent), Italy (5 percent), and both the Netherlands and the United Kingdom at about 4 percent. All of these countries are EU members and, once again, none of Portugal's former colonies are leading sources for imported goods. This may begin to change, as resource-rich Brazil and Portugal are stepping up trade activities. Portugal's EU membership may entice Brazil to send more products through Portugal as an entry point to the European Union's markets.

The EU is working to help Portugal in other ways. For example, Spain and Portugal are working on a plan to construct two high-speed trains that will further link the countries. One train will connect Madrid and Lisbon, the capitals of the two countries, on a route that will only take three hours. A second would connect the cities of Vigo and Porto, with a speedy trip that would only take one hour. EU community funds will finance the project.

IMPACT OF THE ECONOMY ON PORTUGUESE LAND AND PEOPLE

In the mid-twentieth century, the economy was planned and controlled by the government. However, in recent decades, the Portuguese people have benefited from a free-market economy within a democratic governance structure. The change has been quite dramatic. For example, in 1976, the per-capita GDP was only $1,308 per person. In contrast, the per-capita GDP 30 years later, in 2006, was nearly $20,000. Even with these advances, salaries are still lower than in much of the EU.

Problems still exist, though. These include a literacy rate that is lower than most of the EU. Nearly 7 percent of the population is unable to read or write. The quality of education remains a major problem that needs to be addressed. Unemployment also remains a big issue, with a rate that stood at 7.6 percent in late 2006.

The economy of the country and its people also has an impact on the natural environment. Some industries, like tourism, are environmentally friendly. Others, like mining, can have a significant impact if care is not taken in the industry to create protective measures. Environmental challenges currently facing Portugal include soil erosion, air pollution caused by industrial and vehicle emissions, and the problem of water pollution in coastal areas.

Portugal's economic engine has been gaining strength in recent decades. A stable government, the move to a freer marketplace, and membership in the European Union has helped the country to advance rapidly. Even with this growth, there is still an economic gap between Portugal and other EU members. The gap, however, has narrowed considerably during recent years. For centuries, the sea has served as a major element in Portugal's quest for economic development. This dependence continues today, even as the Portuguese turn to the sea to use wave action to generate electrical power. Once again, the sea is helping to provide the potential for a brighter economic future for Portugal. The next chapter will introduce the Portuguese people and the way of life they enjoy today.

7

Living in Portugal Today

This chapter will introduce the Portuguese people and reveal more about who they are, how they live, and what they do during the course of their daily lives. Cultural geographers focus upon the ways of life practiced by various societies. By learning about such traits as ethnicity, language, and religion, it is much easier to understand a country and its people. The same can be said for such common practices as family life, social interactions between and among people, food and dining, entertainment, and the holidays they celebrate.

A CULTURE IN TRANSITION

In many respects, Portugal was the last country in western Europe to begin making the transition from a traditional *folk culture* to a modern, outward-looking *popular culture*. By and large, rural people tend to be isolated, provincial, and often feel threatened by change.

They look to the past, in which they find comfort, much more than focusing on the future, which may appear overwhelming. They are highly self-sufficient and produce most, if not all of what they need. In a family, the husband traditionally built the structure in which the family lived, the mother made the clothes the family wore, and all members of the family joined in to produce the food they ate. Goods they were unable to produce or otherwise provide for themselves were obtained through bartering (trade).

During the eighteenth century, the Industrial Revolution got underway in northwestern Europe. Longstanding traditional ways of living began to change, in some areas more rapidly than in others. With manufacturing came a rapid expansion of trade and commerce, a cash economy, and urbanization. City life brought demands not dreamed of by traditional, rural, folk societies. For example, in order to be successful in an urban environment, one must be able to read, write, and perform basic mathematical functions. Those who lived in urban areas began to work at wage-paying jobs, many of which demanded that workers become highly specialized in what they did. With specialization comes practice and greater expertise. Urban living also requires many services—teachers, health specialists, people involved with sanitation, and countless others. With the spread of popular culture, many countries, including Portugal, became culturally divided. Change came rapidly to the urban population. In the countryside, however, rural populations remained largely traditional.

During much of the twentieth century, Portugal continued to be western Europe's poorest and least-developed country. Particularly in the countryside and small villages, life changed little from generation to generation. It was in the cities where people were caught up in a whirlwind of cultural change. Ideas from distant lands flowed into Lisbon, Porto, and other coastal port cities; so, too, did strange and exotic materials from countries throughout much of the world. Soon, city people began to welcome change, rather than feel threatened by it. After all, many of the new traits made their lives better. New ideas included developments in architecture, theater, the arts and crafts, and education. Although most Portuguese have successfully made the transition from folk to popular culture, islands of rural poverty and traditional ways of living remain. Of course, to a visitor, these folkways can offer a charming variety in the celebration of cultural diversity.

ETHNICITY

Portugal's population, according to the Library of Congress Country Study on Portugal, is "Remarkably homogeneous and [has] been so for all of its history. This lack of ethnic variety helped it become the first unified nation-state in Western Europe." The country study further notes, "For centuries Portugal had virtually no ethnic, tribal, racial, religious, or cultural minorities. Almost all Portuguese spoke the national language, almost all were Roman Catholic, and almost all identified with Portuguese culture and the nation of Portugal." Portugal, in other words, is one of the world's most culturally homogeneous countries. The Portuguese people tend to look, think, communicate, worship, and act in a similar cultural manner.

A nation-state is the territory occupied by a nationality of people (a nation) that also is self-governed (a state). The best way to identify a nation-state is to look for a match between the country's name and that of its common tongue. Nationalities of people almost always are unified by their language. For example, English, French, and German are the respective languages spoken by the English, French, and Germans. If the language and nationality are the same as the country (perhaps with minor alterations), a nation-state is said to exist. England, France, and Germany, then, are nation-states; so is Portugal (a state, or country), the homeland territory occupied by the Portuguese people (a nationality unified by their common tongue). Nation-states are generally quite cohesive and

Portugal is known for its homogenous population: approximately 98 percent of its people are of Mediterranean stock. Pictured here are three Portuguese boys dressed in traditional clothing in Lisbon.

politically stable, simply because people share a common heritage, culture, and values.

In some respects, Portugal's ethnic homogeneity is rather surprising. The country, after all, was one of the world's great maritime powers for a span of several centuries. It was also one of the world's great colonial powers, with holdings that spanned much of the globe. Both conditions might lead one to believe that Portugal would attract a variety of peoples from throughout the world—as did most seafaring countries with vast colonial holdings. But this never happened. During the peak of its power, the majority of the wealth was held by only a handful of people, leaving most Portuguese poor. The country's economy languished and people from foreign lands saw little incentive to leave their own homelands to settle in a country wracked by poverty. Additionally, it was very difficult for outsiders to break ethnic barriers, be accepted, and "find a home" in such an overwhelmingly homogeneous Portuguese society.

Physical geography played a role as well. For thousands of years, the European continent has been an open corridor for human migration. Portugal, however, was at the end of the line; it was a cul-de-sac located at the far tip of the continent lying beyond the huge (even today) natural barrier formed by the Pyrenees Mountains. Migrating peoples saw little reason to venture westward into the tip of the Iberian Peninsula.

Portugal does have several small minority groups. There are as many as 100,000 Gypsies, most of whom live a seminomadic existence in the southern province of Algarve. Perhaps another 100,000 people from elsewhere in Europe now live in Portugal, primarily in Lisbon, Porto, and other cities, or in the Azores or Madeira Islands. Finally, another estimated 100,000 or so people from Portugal's former colonies have settled in the country. None of these groups have been successfully assimilated into Portugal's social and cultural mainstream. Today, an estimated 95 percent of the Portuguese population claims Portuguese national and ethnic identity. Few of the world's countries can match Portugal's level of ethnic homogeneity.

LANGUAGE AND RELIGION

Portuguese, a Latin-derived Romance tongue, is the country's official language and is spoken by nearly everyone. In the northeastern corner of the country, about 5,000 people speak Mirandese, which also was elevated to the status of official language in the late 1990s. Many Portuguese, particularly those living along the border with Spain, speak Spanish as a second language. Most highly educated Portuguese—particularly those involved in international trade and commerce, or with tourism—are multilingual, speaking French, English, or some other European tongue. Many immigrants from former colonies continue to speak their native language if different than Portuguese.

Nearly 94 percent of all Portuguese consider themselves to be Roman Catholic, although many of them are nonpracticing. The trend of less involvement in one's religion is evident

Roman Catholicism is Portugal's primary faith: approximately 94 percent of its citizens consider themselves Catholic. The country is home to one of the world's holiest shrines—Fátima, which is located in central Portugal. Pictured here are Portuguese Army officers carrying the statue of Our Lady of Fátima during the 80th anniversary of the first sighting of the Virgin of the Rosary.

throughout Europe, which has the world's most secular (non-religious) population. People in the northern part of the country tend to be much more devout than those in the south. City dwellers, as is true worldwide, are the least religious.

Portugal, however, is home to one of the world's great religious shrines, the holy site in Fátima, a small community located about 80 miles (130 kilometers) north of Lisbon. Millions of visitors from throughout the world go to Fátima each year to worship at what has become one of Roman Catholicism's most sacred sites. In 1917, the Virgin Mary is said to have appeared five times to three young children who were herding sheep near the community. Supposedly, she made various predictions, including World War II and the spread of Communism. Word of the sightings spread rapidly. By mid-October of that year, some 70,000 faithful gathered to witness a miracle promised by Mary. As the story is told, it was a very stormy day and rain was falling in torrents. Suddenly, the clouds parted and the sun hovered overhead, looking like a dull gray disc, which people could look directly at without discomfort or damage to the eyes. Soon the sun returned to normal and after the drenching rain, people in the assembled crowd realized that they were completely dry. Today, many believers make the pilgrimage to Fátima in the hope of being cured of various illnesses or other infirmities.

Since 1976, the constitution of Portugal has guaranteed freedom of religion to followers of all faiths. Today, there are small numbers of Jews, Protestants (about 1 percent of the population), and non-Christians, including Muslims and animists (those who believe that nonhuman animals and/or inanimate objects possess spirits) from former African colonies.

GENERAL CHARACTERISTICS OF THE PEOPLE

The United Nations ranks countries by what is called a Human Development Index (HDI). The index takes into consideration such factors as life expectancy, literacy, economy, and standard of living. In 2006, Portugal ranked twenty-seventh among 177 countries. By world standards, this position is excellent. However, its position ranks dead last among the countries of western Europe. France, Italy, and Spain, for example, rank sixteenth, seventeenth, and nineteenth, respectively, well above Portugal. What is most significant is that Portugal has made remarkable improvements in its position since the rankings began. In 1990, the first year of the HDI, the country ranked thirty-sixth.

Education

About 93 percent of all Portuguese are literate, or able to read and write. Again, among the world's countries, this figure is high but it ranks below that of all the other countries of western Europe. But here, too, there has been marked improvement during recent decades. In 1970, for example, only 79 percent of the population was literate. Education is mandatory for all children between the ages of 6 and 14 (up to ninth grade). Following their elementary school education, most young people attend three years of high school. Public education is free, and many private schools also attract students, who must pay tuition. Upon graduation, students have the option of attending vocational schools or one of the country's 18 universities. Admission to universities is limited and highly competitive. Students must pay tuition and other fees. The University of Coimbra, founded in 1290, is one of the oldest in Europe.

Health

Life expectancy is a good measure of health. At birth, Portuguese can expect to live about 78 years, a longevity that measures up favorably with other western European countries. The government subsidizes health care and a national health system includes a network of clinics and hospitals scattered throughout the country. These facilities charge fees according to the financial means of their patients. There are also private hospitals and physicians available for those who are willing and able to pay for their services.

TRANSPORTATION AND COMMUNICATION

A country's transportation and communication infrastructure (linkages) generally reflect its economic well-being. As one might expect, in both categories Portugal lags somewhat behind many other European countries. The country has a good network of roads, but lacks the modern superhighways found throughout the European Union. Poor roads and characteristically bad drivers combine to give Portugal one of Europe's highest highway accident fatality rates. Most of the country also is linked by a network of railroads that provide both passenger and freight service. Most cities are linked by domestic commercial airline service. Lisbon is the primary hub for international airline travel, with scheduled flights to all major destinations throughout the world. TAP Portugal is the country's international carrier.

Portugal has a very good network of communications. Amazingly, there are more cell phones in the country than there are people. Radio and television broadcasts reach all parts of the country and nearly 75 percent of the population uses the Internet. Portugal's affiliation with the European Union has been an extremely important factor in the rapid development of both transportation and communication links.

LIFESTYLES AND ACTIVITIES

The Portuguese, much like North Americans and others throughout the world, enjoy holidays, participate in sports and recreational activities, enjoy dining and have preferred foods and beverages, and appreciate the arts.

Holidays

The Portuguese celebrate many holidays. Some are religious occasions, such as Good Friday and Easter (in the spring), the

Feast of the Assumption of the Virgin Mary (in August), All Saints' Day (in the autumn), and the Feast of the Immaculate Conception and Christmas (both in December). There are also national holidays. These include Freedom Day (April), which commemorates the country's overthrow of a dictatorial government, paving the way for democracy; Labor Day (May), during which parades and speeches recognize the contributions of workers; Portugal Day (June), celebrating Luis de Cames, a revered poet; Independence Day (October 5), celebrating the founding of the republic; and Restoration of Independence (December 1). Various cities and regions of Portugal also observe their own special holidays. On most, if not all of these occasions, businesses and other services are closed. In Portugal as elsewhere, holidays are a time for families and friends to gather and celebrate.

Sports and Recreation

In Portugal, as well as throughout much of the world beyond the United States, soccer (called *fútbol*) is not only a sport— it is an obsession. Whether played in a huge stadium before a packed crowd or on the dirt streets of a small village, everyone in Portugal seems to either watch or play the fast-action game. In 2006, Portugal ranked eighth in the world in soccer. The country is considering a bid to host the 2018 World Cup, which by any measure is one of the world's most popular sporting competitions. Basketball also is gaining in popularity.

Bull fighting is popular, too. In Portugal, this sport is done with a twist. Unlike in other countries where it is popular, such as Spain, the bullfighter is mounted on horseback and the bull is not killed.

Recreational activities are similar to those with which most readers are familiar. Picnics, hikes, and enjoying the beach during summer months are all popular. In cities, numerous parks, cafes, theaters, and nightclubs all offer recreational opportunities.

The Portuguese are no different than other Europeans in their love of soccer. Here, fans celebrate in Alveiro, Portugal, after the Portuguese national team qualified for the 2006 World Cup. Portugal advanced all the way to the semifinals, where the team was defeated by France, 1-0.

The Arts

Portuguese arts reflect the country's history, blending Mediterranean (particularly Roman) and Moorish influences. This is particularly true in regard to the country's grand architecture. A visitor is bound to be impressed by the many magnificent churches and cathedrals, castles and palaces, and government buildings. Many buildings, ranging from grand to common, are decorated with *azulejos,* cobalt blue and white glazed tiles. During the colonial era, various Oriental, African, and Brazilian themes were introduced to further enrich the country's arts and crafts.

In discussing the arts, it is important once again to recognize the distinction between traditional folk arts and crafts and those of contemporary popular culture. Portugal is rich in both traditions. Folk music, dance, dress, and art still thrive in remote villages and are showcased in many regional festivals. Today, the country recognizes the importance of its artistic traditions and actively attempts to preserve many of its folkways and promote them as tourist attractions. The visitor to Portugal, and particularly to Lisbon, will surely want to see some of the country's many museums, art galleries, and libraries. Of particular interest to some may be Lisbon's National Coach Museum, which displays Europe's largest collection of coaches.

Of Portugal's traditional folk arts, perhaps none has gained greater attention than has *fado*. This sorrowful, melancholic musical style is similar to North American blues or traditional American country music. Fado first flourished in the working-class streets of Lisbon. Vocals, accompanied by guitars, most often wrap around sad lyrics related to such themes as hard times, down-and-out luck, and romance gone sour. Today, Ana Moura, best known perhaps for her song "Keep My Life in Your Hand," is a very popular young singer of this musical tradition.

Dining and Diet

It is often said, "we are what we eat." Actually, the opposite holds true as well in a cultural sense: "We eat what we are." Food traditions are one of the most deeply entrenched of all cultural practices. Few things that humans do can better illuminate many aspects of their fundamental ways of life. What they eat reveals local crops, tastes and preferences, and historical linkages to other lands and peoples. How and by whom food is prepared can disclose important aspects of culture ranging from technology to social relationships. How the food is eaten, when and how often people dine, and who sits at the table also are revealing. What people drink with their meals varies greatly from culture to culture. Few culture traits can better expose the division between folk and popular culture than does food. It is little wonder that many geographers look to dining and diet when seeking to better understand a people and their cultural variations, associations, and regional patterns.

Portuguese enjoy dining at home and most families seldom eat out. Traditionally, at least, dining is an important occasion. Families gather around the table to enjoy a leisurely meal and converse. Meals may take an hour or more, making them important social, as well as dining, occasions. Particularly in cities, breakfast may be a hastily eaten sandwich, piece of toast, or fruit, washed down with coffee or milk. Dinner, as is true in many rural cultures, is traditionally the main meal of the day and is eaten at midday. ("Dinner" is the main meal of the day; in those cultures eating the main meal in the evening, the smaller noonday meal is referred to as "lunch.") Following the meal, many people enjoy a short afternoon nap, called the *sesta* in Portuguese (*siesta* in Spanish-speaking countries). The evening meal, as is common throughout much of the Mediterranean region and Latin America, is light and eaten late, usually between 8:00 and 9:00 P.M.

Food in Portugal is a blend of Iberian and international influences. Its Mediterranean roots are evident in the country's dietary staples. They include seafood and meat; bread and cheese; many vegetables, including onions and garlic; a variety of fruits; and the extensive use of olive oil. Foreign influences are evident, particularly in spices. Curry, for example, was introduced from the former colony of Goa (in India), as was peri-peri, a fiery Brazilian spice made from chili peppers.

As one would expect in a country that has always looked seaward, Portugal is famous for its seafood. There are many varieties of fish, but none is more popular than *bacalhau*, or dried salt codfish. Before refrigeration, it was difficult to preserve fish and other meats. Codfish, in particular, were caught in abundance—as far away as the Canada's Grand Banks—and preserved by drying and salting the flesh. It is said that there are 365 Portuguese salt cod recipes, one for every day of the year. Various regions of the country have their own cod specialties.

In the south, cod is often combined with scrambled eggs, pota-toes, onions, and spices. In the north, around Porto, a casserole made of cod, potatoes, and onions is considered a national dish. Often, it is mixed with vegetables or garbanzo beans. Shellfish include mussels, clams, and snails. Crabs, squid, and shrimp also are abundant and popular. These and other marine delicacies make Portugal a seafood lover's paradise.

Beef, pork, and poultry also are popular and prepared in many ways. One widely prepared dish includes beef, pork, sausage, vegetables, and spices. Another is *caldo verde*, a green broth made with cabbage, potatoes, and a slice of sausage. This popular soup also has become a national dish. Portugal is famous for its cakes, cookies, and other delicious desserts, too. As is true throughout much of Europe and particularly in the Mediterranean region, wine is consumed by most adults, par-ticularly with the evening meal.

The Mediterranean diet—consisting of various meats and seafood, vegetables, fruits, bread, and cheese, with olive oil widely used in cooking and on salads—is very healthy. The healthy diet is reflected in the longevity of the region's people and also in the fact that obesity has only recently become a problem. This growing health risk appears to be associated with the increasing acceptance of American dining practices. More and more, many Portuguese consume fast food, added sugar, and soft drinks, and are served larger portions. This is just one of many changes that have come to Portugal during recent decades.

8

Portugal Looks Ahead

As Yogi Berra, former catcher and manager of the New York Yankees, once supposedly quipped, "It's hard to predict the future, because it hasn't happened yet." Looking to the past, however, often reveals guideposts that can provide hints of the future. It is hoped that the Portuguese people and their government have learned from past hardships and other experiences. Today, perhaps more than at any time in its history, there are reasons for optimism as Portugal looks ahead to the future. This final chapter will take a systematic look at each of the topics discussed previously and attempt to project the country's future.

PHYSICAL ENVIRONMENT

A variety of natural hazards will continue to plague Portugal. Certainly both the mainland and the island possessions may once again experience the devastation of seismic activity. Earthquakes and other catastrophic events can cause tsunamis, a thunderous rush of water that can destroy everything in its path as it slams ashore. In the Atlantic Ocean, the Madeira and Azores archipelagos will continue to be affected by occasional hurricanes. Droughts and floods will continue to ravage the land from time to time. During the parched summer season, the tinder-dry Mediterranean vegetation will continue to fuel destructive fires. Nature, for the most part, is relatively constant and predictable. Humans and their patterns of settlement and land-use practices are the major variable. For example, a marked increase in coastal settlement makes people more vulnerable to tsunamis and river-delta flooding; so, too, does living in wooded areas expose people to the threat of fire. Spreading agriculture in areas of marginal precipitation makes droughts more severe. Finally, as industry and automobile transportation increase, pollution also will expand unless deliberate steps are taken to curb it.

PORTUGUESE HISTORY

As has been discussed in several sections of this book, Portugal can look back upon a sometimes glorious, yet frequently turbulent past. With Prince Henry's leadership, the country played a significant role in the European voyages of discovery. Following in the footsteps of these courageous early explorers, the country colonized lands in South America, Africa, and Asia. In fact, at its peak, the Portuguese Empire in both area and population was more than 160 times larger than the country itself. Vast wealth flowed into Portugal from Brazil, several lands in Africa, and colonies on the coasts of India and China. Portuguese traders plied the world's seas and their ships were common sights in the world's busiest ports. But prosperity was not widespread; instead, wealth filled the coffers of the nobility and just a small handful of others. Lisbon became a world-class city, but most people lived in rural villages, where they remained isolated, poor, and uneducated as they toiled simply to survive.

Portugal's decline did not occur overnight. It came gradually throughout a span of centuries and resulted from many causes. By the late fifteenth century, the country had keen competition from other European seafaring countries. The French, Dutch, Spanish, British, and others were engaged in colonial expansion and competition for lucrative trade arrangements and routes. Portugal's fortunes went from "feast" to "famine." In the late 1500s, its ruling family was perhaps the richest in the world, yet by 1892, the country was bankrupt. Throughout the centuries, foreign invasion, devastating disease, poor leadership and governance, the loss of colonies, and natural disasters combined to take their toll on the country's well-being. Certainly the 1755 earthquake that destroyed Lisbon and the surrounding communities struck deeply into the very heart and soul of the country; so, too, did the loss of its colonies, which occurred during a span of about 150 years. It is hoped that Portugal has survived the worst of times and has also learned from its experiences.

POPULATION AND SETTLEMENT

Portugal's population is steady. In fact, if current trends continue, it will soon begin to decline. A diminished labor force and a rapidly aging population can only be replaced by an increase in immigration. But many Portuguese are concerned over who these immigrants will be and what effect they will have on the relatively homogeneous Portuguese ethnicity and culture. Judging from trends of recent decades, a continuing rural-to-urban migration will cause cities to swell and drain the countryside of people.

GOVERNMENT

After centuries of often despotic totalitarian government, Portugal finally turned to democracy in 1976. During the past three decades, a constitutional government has ruled the country. Good government is perhaps the single most essential factor contributing to social and economic well-being. All signs point to continued democratic rule and the benefits that come with it.

ECONOMY

Portugal's economy, once the poorest in all of western Europe, is now robust. The transition from a subsistence folk economy based on barter exchange and self-sufficiency to a modern commercial economy is largely completed. Today, most Portuguese are employed in industry or in providing services. As is true in all developed countries, the great majority of people (about two-thirds of them) are engaged in the post-industrial service sector. Since joining the European Union (EU) in 1986, the economy has both diversified and boomed. Recently, the EU invested an additional 3 billion euros (about U.S. $4 billion in 2007) to support new projects to further boost Portugal's economy. All indicators suggest that the country's economy will continue to grow and that its people will continue to enjoy increased prosperity.

CULTURE

With the transition from folk to popular culture comes the acceptance of increasing globalization. Today, through trade, travel, the media, and other means, Portugal is deeply imbedded in a rapidly expanding global culture. Some people are concerned over the possibility that globalization will lead to a bland cultural sameness worldwide. Nothing could be further from the truth. Globalization increases people's options and enriches their cultures. Today, a young person in Lisbon may have an African banana for breakfast, washed down with coffee from Central America. He may have a quick lunch purchased at an American fast food franchise. And he may enjoy listening to the latest hit by a British rock group while dancing steps that originated in Brazil. Media, clothing, food items, tools and

Despite our ever-shrinking world, the Portuguese take pride in their heritage and culture and will continue to celebrate its uniqueness. Here, two Portuguese girls dressed in traditional clothing pose outside a building in the town of Barcelos.

equipment, and so many other products used daily come from lands throughout the world. Today, Portugal and its people remain very proud of their culture and heritage. For perhaps the first time in history, they can look to the future with enthusiasm and optimism. Most if not all of the pieces are in place to ensure that their lives will continue to improve.

Physical Geography

Location Southwestern Europe, occupying western edge of Iberian Peninsula, bordering Spain and the Atlantic Ocean; westernmost country of mainland Europe

Area Total: 35,672 square miles (92,391 square kilometers) [about the size of Indiana]; *land:* 35,503 square miles (91,951 square kilometers); *water:* 170 square miles (440 square kilometers) *note:* area includes Azores and Madeira islands

Boundaries *Border country:* Spain; *land:* 754 miles (1,214 kilometers); *water* (Atlantic Ocean): 1,114 miles (1,793 kilometers)

Climate Mediterranean sub-tropical with maritime temperate conditions; cool and rainy in north, warmer and drier in south (similar to coastal California)

Terrain Mountainous, plateaus, valleys north of the Tagus River; rolling plains and broad river valleys

Elevation Extremes Lowest point is Atlantic Ocean (sea level); highest point is Ponta do Pico (Pico or Pico Alto) on Ilha do Pico in the Azores, 7,713 feet (2,351 meters)

Land Use Arable land, 17.29%; permanent crops, 7.84%; other, 4.87% (2005)

Irrigated Land 2,510 square miles (6,500 square kilometers) (2003)

Natural Hazards Earthquakes; severe fires during summer months

Natural Resources Fish; forests (cork); minerals: iron ore, copper, zinc, tin, tungsten, silver, gold, uranium, marble, clay, gypsum, salt; arable land; hydropower

Environmental Issues Soil erosion; air pollution caused by industrial and vehicle emissions; water pollution, especially in coastal areas; factory wastes; deforestation; soil erosion; wildlife populations threatened by illegal hunting

People

Population 10,605,870 (July 2006 est.); males, 5,152,048 (2006 est.); females, 5,453,822 (2006 est.)

Population Density 300 per square mile (116 per square kilometer)

Population Growth Rate 0.36%, nearly all of which is the result of in-migration (2006 est.)

Net Migration Rate	3.4 migrants/1,000 population (2006 est.)
Fertility Rate	1.47 children born/woman (2006 est.)
Birthrate	10.7 births/1,000 population
Death Rate	10.5 deaths/1,000 population
Life Expectancy at Birth	Total population: 77.7 years; male, 74.4 years; female, 81.2 years (2006 est.)
Median Age	38.5 years; male, 36.4 years; female, 40.6 years (2006 est.)
Ethnic Groups	98% homogeneous Mediterranean; fewer than 100,000 citizens of black African descent who immigrated to mainland during decolonization; since 1990, a small number of East Europeans have entered Portugal
Religion	Roman Catholic (94%)
Percent Urban/Rural	53% urban (approximately 25% of whom live in the Lisbon metropolitan area); 47% rural
Languages	Portuguese (official); Mirandese (official, but spoken by only about 5,000 people living in northeastern Portugal)
Literacy	(Age 15 and over can read and write) Total population: 93.3% (male, 95.5%; female, 91.3%) (2003 est.)

Economy

Currency	Euro
GDP Purchasing Power Parity (PPP)	$205 billion (2006 est.)
GDP Per Capita	$19,100 (2006 est.)
Labor Force	5.52 million (2005 est.)
Unemployment	7.6% (2006 est.)
Labor Force by Occupation	Services, 60%; industry, 30%; agriculture, 10%
Agricultural Products	*Crops:* grain, potatoes, tomatoes, olives, grapes; *Animal products:* sheep, cattle, goats, swine, poultry, dairy products, fish
Industries	Textiles and footwear; wood pulp, paper, and cork; metals and metalworking; oil refining; chemicals; fish canning; rubber and plastic products; ceramics; electronics and communications equipment; rail transportation equipment; aerospace equipment; ship construction and refurbishment; wine; tourism
Exports	$46.8 billion f.o.b. (2006 est.)
Imports	$67.7 billion f.o.b. (2006 est.)

Leading Trade Partners	Exports: Spain, 25.9%; France, 13.1%; Germany, 11.9%; UK, 8%; U.S., 5.4%; Italy, 4.3% (2005). Imports: Spain, 29%; Germany, 13.4%; France, 8.5%; Italy, 5.2%; Netherlands, 4.3%; UK, 4.2%
Export Commodities	Clothing and footwear; machinery; chemicals; cork and paper products; hides
Import Commodities	Machinery and transport equipment; chemicals; petroleum; textiles; agricultural products
Transportation	Roadways: 48,759 miles (78,470 kilometers), of which 41,933 miles (67,484 kilometers) are paved (2003); Railways: 1,771 miles (2,850 kilometers); Airports: 66–43 are paved runways (2006); Waterways: 130 miles (210 kilometers) on Douro River from Porto

Government

Country Name	Conventional long form: Portuguese Republic; Conventional short form: Portugal; Local long form: Republica Portuguesa; Local short form: Portugal
Capital City	Lisbon
Type of Government	Parliamentary democracy
Head of Government:	Prime Minister Jose Socrates (since March 12, 2005)
Independence	1143 (Kingdom of Portugal recognized); October 5, 1910 (independent republic proclaimed)
Administrative Divisions	18 districts and two autonomous regions

Communications

TV Stations	62 (2006)
Radio Stations	219
Phones	(Line) 4,234,000 million (2005); (cell) 11,448,000 million
Internet Users	About 7.8 million (2006)

* Source: *CIA-The World Factbook* (2006)

History at a Glance

500,000 B.C.	Earliest traces of humans in Portugal.
22,500	End of Neanderthal era in Portugal.
3000	Agricultural societies emerge in Portugal.
2000	Cultural variations begin to appear in neolithic cultures in Portugal.
1200	Phoenicians settle the area of present-day Lisbon.
800	Celts arrive in Portugal from central Europe.
60	Julius Caesar enters Portugal with a huge army; this begins 500 years of Roman rule.
A.D. 406	Germanic tribes move into the Iberian Peninsula.
710	Moors conduct their first successful attack on the Iberian Peninsula across the Strait of Gibraltar.
711	Tariq ibn Ziyad attacks at the Rock of Gibraltar with a Moor army of 12,000.
718	Moors control most of the Iberian Peninsula.
1128	Afonso Henriques establishes Portugal's first royal family, called the House of Burgundy.
1139	Afonso Henriques leads a victory over the Moors in the battle of Ourique.
1143	Treaty of Zamora recognizes Portugal's independence from León and Castile (present-day Spain).
1147	King Afonso I, with assistance from Catholic crusaders, defeats the Moors and drives them out of Lisbon.
1185	King Afonso I dies.
1249	Last Moors in Portugal are driven out of the city of Faro.
1312	Knights Templar disbanded.
1318	Order of Our Lord Jesus Christ formed by King Denis.
1325	King Denis dies; succeeded by Afonso IV (1325–1357).
1348–49	Black Death (the plague) arrives and kills a third of the Portuguese population.
1373	Treaty of Alliance signed with England.
1386	Treaty of Windsor signed with England.
1387	King João marries an English woman named Philippa of Lancaster.
1394	Prince Henry "The Navigator" is born to Philippa and King João.
1411	Portuguese win a major military victory over Castile in the Battle of Aljubarrota.

1418	Prince Henry establishes a school at Sagres for navigation, mapmaking, and shipbuilding.
1455	Prince Henry prohibits the capturing of slaves.
1460	Prince Henry dies.
1488	By sailing around the southern tip of Africa, Bartolomeu Dias proves that the Atlantic and Indian oceans are connected.
1494	The Treaty of Tordesillas divides the world between the Spanish and Portuguese.
1497	Vasco da Gama becomes the first to travel by sea from Portugal to India.
1500	Pedro Álvares Cabral sails on the second Portuguese expedition to India.
1521	Magellan is killed in the Philippines; his crew becomes first to circumnavigate the world.
1568	Sebastião becomes king.
1578	King Sebastião conducts an unsuccessful invasion of the Moors in Morocco.
Late 16th century	Portugal's royal family (Sebastião) is believed to be the world's richest.
1580	Spain invades and annexes Portugal.
1640	Portugal successfully rebels against Spanish rule.
1755	Lisbon is destroyed on All Saints' Day by severe earthquake, followed by a tsunami and fire that kills as many as 100,000 people and leaves 85 percent of the city in ruin.
1807	Napoleon and Spain invade Portugal and seize Lisbon.
1810	Portuguese successfully repel the third French invasion.
1822	João VI vows to uphold the new constitution, creating a constitutional monarchy; Brazil declares its independence from Portugal.
1892	Portugal declares bankruptcy.
1908	King Carlos is assassinated by antiroyalists.
1916	Portugal joins the Allies in World War I.
1917	Three young girls claim to have been visited by the Virgin Mary outside the village of Fátima; in October of that year, 70,000 witness the "Miracle of the Sun."
1918	President Sidónio Pais is killed.

1926	Military coup overthrows the democratic government; start of ascent of António de Oliveira Salazar's dictatorial rule.
1968	António de Oliveira Salazar has a stroke after 40 years of rule; Marcelo Caetano assumes leadership.
1974	A coup overthrows Caetano, paving the way for a democratic government.
1976	Portugal's democratic constitution adopted; Second Republic begins.
1977	Major copper and tin deposit is discovered at Neves-Corvo.
1986	Portugal enters the European Community (later called the European Union, or EU).
1998	The Alentejo Dam is built on the Guadiana River.
2002	Euro replaces the escudo as Portugal's official currency.
2005	Parliamentary elections conducted; the Portuguese Socialist Party wins 45 percent of vote and 121 of 230 Assembly of the Republic seats; Constitution revised for seventh time.
2006–2007	Introduction of wave technology for electricity generation.

Anderson, James M. *The History of Portugal.* Westport, Conn.: Greenwood Press, 2000.

Barrett, Pam, ed. *Insight Guide: Portugal.* Maspeth, N.Y.: Langenscheidt Publishers, 1999.

Brown, Jules, Mark Ellingham, John Fisher, Matthew Hancock, and Graham Kenyon. *Rough Guide to Portugal.* 11th ed. New York: Rough Guides, 2005.

Carter, Terry, and Laura Dunston. *Best of Lisbon.* Oakland, Calif.: Lonely Planet Publications, 2006.

CultureGrams. *Portugal.* Ann Arbor, Mich.: ProQuest (annual editions)

Folkard, Claire, and Ferdie McDonald, eds. *Lisbon.* Eyewitness Travel Guides. New York: DK Publishing, Inc., 1997.

Kaplan, Marion. *The Portuguese: The Land and Its People.* London: Viking, 1991.

Konstam, Angus. *Historical Atlas of Exploration: 1492–1600.* New York: Checkmark Books, an imprint of Facts on File, Inc., 2000.

Poelzl, Volker. *Culture Shock: Portugal.* Portland, Ore.: Graphic Arts Center Publishing Company, 2004.

Porter, Darwin, and Danforth Prince. *Frommer's Portugal.* New York: Macmillan Company, 2006.

Russell-Wood, A. J. R. *The Portuguese Empire, 1415–1808: A World on the Move.* Baltimore: Johns Hopkins University Press, 1998.

Tranaeus, Tomas, Jane Ewart, and Michelle de Larrabeiti, eds. *Portugal.* Eyewitness Travel Guides. New York: DK Travel, 2003.

Further Reading

Books

Birmingham, David. *A Concise History of Portugal.* Cambridge, UK: Cambridge University Press, 2003.

Carreiro, Carlos B. *Portugal's Golden Years: The Life and Times of Prince Henry "The Navigator."* Pittsburgh, Pa.: Dorrance Publishing Company, 2006.

Saramago, Jose, Amanda Hopkinson, trans., and Nick Caistor, trans. *Journey to Portugal: In Pursuit of Portugal's History and Culture.* Fort Washington, Pa.: Harvest Books, 2002.

Vincent, Mary, and R. A. Stradling. *Cultural Atlas of Spain and Portugal.* New York: Checkmark Books, 1995.

Web sites

European Union
www.eu2001.se/static/eng/eu_info/medlem_portugal.asp
The official European Union site gives this link to economic data on Portugal.

Portuguese Assembly of the Republic
www.parlamento.pt/ingles/cons_leg/crp_ing/index.html
The text of the 2005 Portuguese Constitution can be found on this, the official site of the Portuguese parliamentary body.

Welcome to Portugal
www.portugal.org
This overview of travel information and Portugal's economy is useful in exploring the country.

Portugal-Info.net
www.portugal-info.net
This site contains a wide variety of information about the geography, economy, present, and past of Portugal.

Virtual Portugal
www.portugalvirtual.pt/_tourism/index.html
Viewers can browse through an extensive guide for visiting Lisbon and Portugal.

Permanent Mission of Portugal to the United Nations
www.un.int/portugal/eng
This Portuguese source (in English) offers a wide range of information about the country.

Index

Index

DOUGLAS A. PHILLIPS is a lifetime educator, writer, and consultant who has worked and traveled in more than 100 countries on six continents. After traveling to his 100th country in 2006, he was admitted to the Traveler's Century Club. During his career, he has worked as a middle school teacher, a curriculum developer, an author, and as a trainer of educators in numerous countries around the world. He has served as the president of the National Council for Geographic Education and has received the Outstanding Service Award from the National Council for the Social Studies, along with numerous other awards. He, his wife, Marlene, and their three children, Chris, Angela, and Daniel, have lived in South Dakota and Alaska in the past. His daughter is now in Texas while he, his wife, and his two sons reside in Arizona, where he writes and serves as an educational consultant for the Center for Civic Education. He and his wife traveled to Portugal in 2006 and they both thoroughly love the people and incredible culture and landscapes of the country.

CHARLES F. GRITZNER is distinguished professor of geography at South Dakota State University in Brookings. He is now in his fifth decade of college teaching, research, and writing. In addition to teaching, he enjoys writing, working with teachers, and sharing his love of geography with readers. As editor for Chelsea House's MODERN WORLD NATIONS and MODERN WORLD CULTURES series, he has a wonderful opportunity to combine each of these "hobbies." Gritzner has served as both president and executive director of the National Council for Geographic Education and has received the council's highest honor, the George J. Miller Award for Distinguished Service to Geographic Education, as well as other honors from the NCGE, Association of American Geographers, and other organizations.